PRAISE FOR CHRI
Step Up and I

Step Up and Play Big *takes you out of your comfort zone and teaches you how easy it is to simply make a choice. Change is constant — society, knowledge, technology, understanding and communications are evolving at the speed of light. As always, "The Coach" imparts his real-world wisdom and experience. The takeaway: the better prepared we are to accept change the happier and more successful we will become.*

STEPHAN LOWY
CEO Lowy's Moving Service, Successful Serial Entrepreneur

As a professional sales leader for the past 25 years, I have discovered this book to be both a wonderful and practical guide to help deal with and understand the new challenges we all face today. It provides a simple and clear road map to help us be more efficient and successful in today's business environment.

HERBERT R. SELANDER, JR.
Former Managing Director, Global Insurance Brokerage

In today's business environment where time is the precious commodity, I look for ideas that are quick to the point, practical, and indicate usefulness that help me manage and grow the business. The information in Step Up and Play Big *fits my pace of life today. There is never enough time — and time pressures create the need for a book that gets to the point, but with enough real-world experience to make it clearly understood and implementable. Chris provides a framework for understanding the key points and then provides a straight line to the heart of the matter: do it — just do it instead of over-thinking the situation and getting paralyzed. The investment price for this book will return so much practical advice and action this year and in the future. Buy it, use it, and let the rest of the world catch up to you.*

DONALD G. McDERMOTT
President, DG McDermott Associates

Chris Ruisi has a unique ability to assess a collaborative exchange of concerns and ideas between business leaders, and then offer a simplistic approach to obtaining solutions or achieving objectives. He is one of the most out-of-the-box-thinking individuals I know, and he always seems to have his finger on the pulse of the needs of the business community. His fundamental philosophy – that the right attitude, and a simple, disciplined game plan can overcome almost any obstacle – is a refreshing alternative to some of the self-help decrees touted by other published writers. Chris makes it easy to see the opportunity in every challenge.

BENJAMIN L. WALDRON
Executive Director, Monmouth (NJ) Ocean Development Council

STEP UP AND PLAY BIG

STEP UP AND PLAY BIG

Unlock Your Potential to Be Exceptional in 8 Simple Steps

CHRIS RUISI

"THE COACH"

Advantage®

Published by Advantage, Charleston, South Carolina.
Member of Advantage Media Group.

ADVANTAGE is a registered trademark and the Advantage colophon is a trademark of Advantage Media Group, Inc.

Printed in the United States of America.

ISBN: 978-1-59932-625-2
LCCN: 2012937635

This publication is designed to provide accurate and authoritative information in regard to the subject matter covered. It is sold with the understanding that the publisher is not engaged in rendering legal, accounting, or other professional services. If legal advice or other expert assistance is required, the services of a competent professional person should be sought.

Advantage Media Group is proud to be a part of the Tree Neutral® program. Tree Neutral offsets the number of trees consumed in the production and printing of this book by taking proactive steps such as planting trees in direct proportion to the number of trees used to print books. To learn more about Tree Neutral, please visit www.treeneutral.com. To learn more about Advantage's commitment to being a responsible steward of the environment, please visit www.advantagefamily.com/green

Advantage Media Group is a leading publisher of business, motivation, and self-help authors. Do you have a manuscript or book idea that you would like to have considered for publication? Please visit www.amgbook.com or call 1.866.775.1696

To Jonah, Olivia, Bennett, Sophia
And Alexa
You make the present fun
And the future
Worth waiting for!

ACKNOWLEDGMENTS

This book could not have been written without the help of many people. Those who deserve very special recognition include: my wife, Paula, who could be held up as an example of all that is good in the world; Mom and Dad, who taught me that a main role for parents is to be cheerleaders for their children while at the same time helping their children stay grounded and focused; our oldest son, Christopher, who has shown me what a genuine, caring person is; our middle son, Stephen, who in the face of a mountain of adversity showed me what real strength and courage is and, as the father of our three grandchildren, has shown me where I could have been a better father; our youngest son, Andrew, who has demonstrated what the real measure of commitment and courage is and who has such great balance in his life that one day many will learn from him; Casey the Wonder Dog (our first-ever golden retriever), Riley Rose, our current golden retriever, and Toby, our Westie, who all knew exactly when a gentle nudge, soft lick, or a cold nose rub was needed to lift one's spirits; my clients, who at times drove me absolutely crazy but gave me the daily motivation and opportunity to help make a difference in their lives.

I also want to thank the many mentors I have been fortunate to have during my career. Among the most notable were Gordon E. Crosby Jr. and George Hoffacker.

Gordon E. Crosby Jr. was the chairman and CEO of USLIFE Corporation and my only boss for the twenty-five years I was blessed to work there. He gave me as many opportunities as I could handle and was always there with a word of encouragement or criticism when needed—and usually deserved. I still remember his words: "Chris, I may let you step off the curb and twist your ankle so you can learn from your mistakes, but I will never let you fall out of a window."

George Hoffacker was actually my very first mentor in my very first job out of college, at Franklin National Bank. George taught me how to look for solutions and find confidence in my decisions. He would deliberately look unapproachable to test how badly I really needed to talk with him. Once I worked up the courage to walk into his office, he had the unique ability to turn every question I had for him back into a question to me. Invariably, this led me to find the answer I was seeking. It is a skill that I use now and hope one day to pass on to others.

*There is no passion to be found playing small, in settling for
a life that is less than the one you are capable of living.*

—Nelson Mandela, eleventh president of South Africa

THE WOUNDED WARRIOR PROJECT

WWW.WOUNDEDWARRIORPROJECT.ORG

ITS MISSION:

To honor and empower wounded warriors

ITS PURPOSE:

To raise awareness and enlist the public's aid
for the needs of injured service members

To help injured service members aid and assist each other

To provide unique, direct programs and services to
meet the needs of injured service members

I made the decision to donate 20 percent of the proceeds from the sales of *Step Up and Play Big* to the Wounded Warrior Project (WWP). My reasons for doing this are simple: First, when our young men or women make the decision to serve, they have taken what I believe is the ultimate action to step up. Second, wherever they may serve, regardless of the role they play, they must realize their full capabilities in order to play big. They always need to bring their "A" game to whatever their mission might be for that day and every day thereafter. You just can't bring your "A" game if you are not committed to doing the best you can. So, my third reason for supporting this organization is to recognize the level of commitment displayed by our men and women who serve. When our heroes are injured, we need to be there to provide the help and support required. Their wounds are the ultimate proof of their commitment to step up and play big. It's my hope that whatever I donate to the WWP will help these warriors find comfort and, more important, a new vision for their future. Finally, our youngest son demonstrated his willingness to step up and play big when he volunteered to serve as a US Navy aviator (Tailhook). My decision to share the proceeds with this organization was influenced also by his brave choice.

REGISTER YOUR BOOK FOR ONGOING LEARNING OPPORTUNITIES AND GET A FREE WORKBOOK

Thank you for your interest in *Step Up and Play Big*. The play-big concept encompasses more than can be captured in just one book. To step up and play big is a lifetime commitment that you make to yourself. By registering your book, you will, on a regular basis, receive up-to-date tips, tactics, and advice to help you continue to play big. This information will include:

- special reports and white papers
- invitations to webinars and teleseminars
- blog posts and articles
- video and audio educational files
- selected e-books

Registering your book involves one very simple step: go to **www.stepupandplaybig.com** and follow the instructions, "Register Your Book."

And, when you do register the book, you will receive absolutely free your own *Step Up and Play Big* workbook—"Creating Your Vision"—that will help you apply the advice and strategies in the book so you can "work the stuff" to benefit you, your business, or your career.

When you register the book, it will be one of the best investments you make in yourself. So, why wait? Make sure that you register your book—today.

CONTENTS

WHY THIS BOOK AND WHY NOW

> ### DON'T STOP LEARNING
> This book is keyed to Leadership and other courses found online at Chris Ruisi's Play Big university at www.**StepUpandPlayBig**.com

With so many self-help books out there, why add to the stack? I like things quick and to the point. It's not a perfect approach, but it works for me. I admire many of the self-help experts whom I have read, but I have found that a fair amount of this information takes a long time to get to the meat of the matter, and I'm not suggesting that all of what I call extra is not without value. I just like to get to the point faster and put what I have read into practice. So, as I prepared to write this book, I was motivated by the belief that there are other get-to-the-pointers out there like me. As such, it was a simple decision to pull all of this together in what I hope is an easy-to-read and understandable approach. The "stuff" works if you "work the stuff."

So why this book? My personal belief is some people spend way too much time thinking and considering versus acting to make something happen. You know, they usually start each sentence with "I hope" or "I am hoping that." My goals in writing this book were, first, to show how to make it easy to bring about the change you want to achieve; second, to outline for you, the reader, certain habits or actions that will help you to be the master of your circumstances, as opposed to being a victim; and third, to show how easy it really is to step up to a higher performance level. Unfortunately, many find it easier to find safety in the middle and then complain about it. One of the most important things I learned during my career is that eventually you have to act. As you might conclude, action is the foundation needed to step up and play big.

COACH SAYS ...

If you don't know how to take action, there is no way you can step up and play big.

Now, I admit that this approach does carry with it a fair number of chances to make some mistakes. But so what? We learn from our mistakes. We don't learn from inaction, or as I often say, from "studying all of the sides of a circle." I often joke, but I half-believe that, each morning when we become vertical, an alarm goes off in our brain that triggers the question, what can I do today to make simple things hard and then, take my time doing them? So, one key take-away from this book is activity gets results. Continue making decisions to move forward. Keep it as simple as you can. Learn as you go. It's a lot more fun and meaningful.

Today's challenges have put us under fire. Being under fire can be intimidating. I know; I've been there, and I learned from it. No experience in sports is the equivalent. But sports offers something the chaos of battle doesn't allow: a chance to gain success by understanding the rules and playing by them, sometimes in ways the other side doesn't expect. So think of being under fire as being down by two points with fifteen seconds to play. Those kinds of challenges can create opportunities for us—if we choose to accept them—to truly demonstrate what we are capable of.

This is what I refer to as our stretch point. When we stretch, we make the decision to increase the limits of our comfort zone and create new benchmarks for our future success. Conversely, when we do not stretch, we try to protect ourselves by setting our personal success bar way too low. By doing so, we cheat ourselves of our full efforts. When this happens, we do not take full advantage of our capabilities and get into the dangerous habit of just doing enough to get by. I have seen this far too many times, and, quite frankly, it makes me mad. I have a hard time rationalizing why someone would deliberately limit his or her growth. Normally, this self-limiting attitude is bad enough, but it is particularly dangerous when we are facing significant challenges, and defeat is possible. It results in derailed careers and may, if left unchecked, be fatal to a career and a business. You can win as long as there is still time on the clock.

Just like the soldiers in the trenches, you must always be prepared for what you might face over the next hill or on the horizon. To be successful and to survive, those soldiers knew that they must keep moving forward, facing risk after risk, to achieve their desired objective. The same is true of a winning team.

Trenches give soldiers temporary protection during which they can think about what got them to that point and how they can use that knowledge to plan their next move forward. Take every opportunity to rethink, replan and re-imagine your way to victory. There is no such thing as "standing still or running in place" in life or in business. Success belongs to those who use the trenches as a staging ground for moving forward, regardless of the risks. Success also belongs to those who see each challenge as an opportunity in disguise.

With the help of what you will read in this book, you can beat any challenge you face. *Step Up and Play Big* was written to help you move forward. The lessons are simple, but the impact can be as significant as you want it to be.

You will not find in this book a business bedtime story or fable. There is no wise old man living in a hut in the woods and coming up with riddles. While there are a few animal references, there are no herds, flocks, mice, penguins, or fish, or anything struggling with change, leadership, or food that has been moved. Finally, there is no struggling executive who works late into the night missing family time while he ponders why he just can't get his act together, or as we used to say back in my old Brooklyn neighborhood, "get his head out of that dark spot." There is just good stuff that works. I know because it did for me. It's really simple stuff because it is my belief that we make it all too complicated.

But the "stuff" works only if you "work the stuff." Vince Lombardi once said, "I have never known a really successful man who deep in his heart did not understand the grind, the discipline it takes to win." To help you stay disciplined in your focus, I have tried to describe each point in as simple a way as possible. Heck! That's how I learned it, so it should work for you also.

So, get started. The game is on, and you have waited far too long. It's your time to step up and play big. Work it!

COACH SAYS …

My keep-it-simple approach was motivated by that famous Greek diner owner named Pete Dionasopolis—a character created by John Belushi—who captured his entire world in just three very simple words: "cheeseburger, cheeseburger, cheeseburger." I'm with you all the way in this book. My role is to be your coach, using what I know and offering ways of stepping up and playing big.

TO STEP UP AND PLAY BIG, START WITH A VISION

DON'T STOP LEARNING

This book is keyed to Leadership and other courses found online at Chris Ruisi's Play Big university at www.**StepUpandPlayBig**.com

Vision without action is a daydream.
Action without a vision is a nightmare.

—JAPANESE PROVERB

ONE OF THE BEST WAYS to overcome the fear of doing something is to be confident in your abilities to handle the task at hand. After all, to move forward, you eventually have to take a risk. The mental process of thinking through this risk is where fear is born. With confidence you can put fear in its place and be able to step up and play big.

So, it stands to reason that if you don't know where you are going—namely, have a vision—there is no way you can properly assess the risk or control the fear. You see how it works?

Let's talk about the importance of having a vision if you are going to successfully step up and play big. Whenever I talk about the importance of having a vision, I am reminded of the words of

Lewis Carroll in *Alice's Adventures in Wonderland* when Alice meets the Cheshire cat sitting in a tree:

> "Would you tell me, please, which way
> I ought to walk from here?"
>
> "That depends a good deal on where
> you want to get to," said the Cat.
>
> "I don't much care where," said Alice.
>
> "Then it doesn't matter which way
> you walk," said the Cat.

The one quality common to all who successfully play big is a clear going-forward vision. These folks understand that they can have complete control of their futures and are focused on being the master of their circumstances as opposed to being a victim of them. They take the time to think through and develop a clear picture of where they or their organizations need to be no more than three years from the present. They then work each day to make their visions a reality. There are, of course, setbacks and barriers. However, the clarity of their vision, perseverance, and self-discipline allow them to push through anything that gets in their way.

STEP UP: Without a vision, there is no way you can have confidence in your abilities to move forward. Running in place and wishing and hoping and waiting become your life.

I have all of my clients visualize in detail the clearest picture of what their business or career will look like three years out. I explain that the more detail the better and that in order to play big they need to think big, aim high, and not be too conservative.

Your vision is the rudder of your ship. Without one you cannot control your direction. You are at the mercy of the wind, the waves, and current. It doesn't matter how much passion you have, you're headed east of nowhere. Without a clear vision, the news and distractions we encounter every day are more likely to bog you down and create more doubt and fear, thereby increasing the likelihood of your being a victim. Without a vision, nothing happens.

I also recommend that when you create your vision you keep these two key points in the forefront of your mind:

1. Don't think of your vision as a rigid, final product with every detail pinned down. Think of it more as a series of guideposts of key topics to focus attention on and targets to aim for; and

2. Regularly review your vision, evaluate it, and revise it. Keep questioning your assumptions. Stay flexible and open to change.

Finally, your vision does not have to be perfect to get started. I recently heard a speaker describe that it can be like driving your car cross-country on a dark road at night, and you can see only as far as the end of the light cast by your headlights. While you can't see very far ahead, and the conditions are far from perfect, you can make the entire trip that way if you stay focused and keep moving forward. Don't let what you can't see hold you back. Create your vision and implement it, and you will take the most important first step to stepping up and playing big. Anything less is just an excuse.

PLAY BIG: Start now. Begin to describe in as much detail as possible what you want your future to look like three years from now, the more detail the better. Think big. Share with those who share your values. Solicit their input to make it even better. (If you registered your book, use the workbook that I provided for this exercise.)

CHAPTER 1

TO STEP UP AND PLAY BIG YOU NEED TO FIND YOUR FULL CAPABILITIES

DON'T STOP LEARNING

This book is keyed to Leadership and other courses found online at Chris Ruisi's Play Big university at www.**StepUpandPlayBig**.com

It sometimes feels very easy to fail. We convince ourselves that it is bad to experience the effects of failure. In reality, depending on how we handle it, from failure we can learn how to do it better.

To protect ourselves from the pain of failure, we deliberately lower our expectations for our own performance. Setting the bar too low doesn't

COACH SAYS ...

Quitting and giving up, not failure, is what needs to be feared.

help or protect us. In fact, by doing so, you cheat yourself of your full effort. You get into the dangerous habit of doing just enough to get by. In other words, you play it safe. Many people would be surprised to learn that it really doesn't take a lot of additional effort to be better than average.

Playing it too safe or doing just enough to get by actually holds you back from using your full capabilities. In essence, when you play it too safe, you sabotage yourself, shrink your capabilities, and derail

> **COACH SAYS ...**
>
> *If you don't experience a setback now and then, you are playing it too safe.*

your career and initiatives. And, when you begin to expect less from yourself, others will notice and expect less from you also. The result: Your career and professional development go into a downward spiral, leaving growth, promotions and success far behind.

Once you get into the habit of limiting your full capabilities, you begin to use with increasing frequency the most deadly and dangerous four-letter word in our daily vocabulary: *can't*. This is when you talk yourself out of doing the things that you think you can't do.

So, what are you going to do to regain control and step

Bench Injuries

How do you know when you are living and working below your full capabilities? Here are some obvious—and not so obvious—signs:

- When confronted with a new challenge or project, you spend more time thinking and worrying about what could go wrong as opposed to the opportunities that can be captured.

- You find it harder and harder to make the necessary decisions to move forward; you start to second-guess yourself at every turn.

- You no longer have that same confidence in yourself that you had in the past.

- You are no longer having fun.

up and play big when it comes to maximizing your full capabilities? Well, for starters you need to focus on improving the habits of self-discipline and perseverance.

Self-discipline helps you focus on your priorities and control your tasks. As you control tasks, you build more self-discipline. As you build more self-discipline, your level of self-confidence develops further. Don't be fooled. Self-discipline is often a very difficult habit to develop and sustain. Personal courage is needed to help you push through the barriers you will face to develop your self-discipline. However, as this skill develops, the more courage you will have to tackle the bigger challenges waiting ahead for you. As this process begins to unfold, you will be moving closer to recognizing and using your full capabilities.

> **COACH SAYS ...**
>
> *This is really what life is all about: every time you solve one challenge, you earn the right to solve a greater one.*

> **COACH SAYS ...**
>
> *Perseverance means never quitting.*

Everyone has a dream or a goal that they would like to accomplish. Oftentimes the difference between accomplishing or not accomplishing the goal is not about how strong our resolve is to overcome the difficulties or obstacles that we face. Rather, it's about whether or not you are maximizing your full capabilities.

We have all faced challenges throughout our business lives. It is at this crucial time that we will make the decision to face the challenge or give up. It is always easier to give up. And by doing so, it becomes even easier to quit the next time another challenge faces us on the road to a different goal. It is in this process of giving up that not using our full capabilities is born and takes root in our mind.

Real limits will not box you in because you can always find a way to deal with them. Rather, the false ones you are carrying around in your mind become the self-imposed prison of your dreams and goals, the tendency to work below your capabilities. You need to set yourself free. You must give yourself permission to take risks. After all, how does a turtle move forward? It's simple: He sticks his neck out.

One of the best examples of someone who would not allow himself to live below his capabilities is that of a young man at a St. Louis high school who had lost his hand at the wrist. When a doctor asked about his handicap, the teenager replied, "I don't have a handicap. I just don't have a right hand." The doctor learned that the young man was one of the leading scorers on his high-school football team.

> ## COACH SAYS ...
>
> *It's time to start focusing on possibilities rather than limits and obstacles. The greatest handicap a person has is not realizing his or her full potential.*

Do you remember that scene in the movie *City Slickers* when Jack Palance raises up his finger and says, "The secret is right here"? In essence, the secret for your success, the key to unlock your full capabilities, is within you. Take responsibility for your life and your success. Stop letting the world get in your way.

In life you cannot have everything. As Mark Twain said, "Where would you put it?" But, you can have whatever level of success you set your sights on. To be successful, you must be willing to embrace change, for as Mark Twain also said, "The only person who likes change is a wet baby."

Change for most of us is hard. When confronted with the need to change, our natural tendency is to stay in our comfort zone and hold on to what we know. We create our own internal barriers, namely, "I can't do that." Now is not the time to add more barriers, especially self-imposed ones. Now is the time to take a risk and challenge yourself to use to the maximum your full capabilities.

PLAY BIG: What's the one skill or talent you want to develop or enhance? Why? How will it improve your performance? What are the steps you will need to follow? By when? Assess your status quo. Build your plan and implement it.

TO STEP UP AND PLAY BIG, YOU HAVE TO FIGHT DISTRACTIONS

DON'T STOP LEARNING

This book is keyed to Leadership and other courses found online at Chris Ruisi's Play Big university at www.**StepUpandPlayBig**.com

Dissatisfaction and discouragement are not caused by the absence of things but the absence of vision.

—Anonymous

Okay, before we go any further, let's huddle here for a minute and ask some big questions.

1. Do you find that during any particular week you waste time and money and still miss opportunities?

If you answered yes, you need to have a vision three years out for your business or career. Without a specific vision, there is no way that you can set realistic goals to move forward. Without specific goals, there is no way you can measure progress.

> ### COACH SAYS ...
> *You can't win if you don't know what and where the goal is.*

Finally, without daily planning and following a ninety-day plan, you will continue to waste time and money until both are gone.

2. Do you find yourself involved in a fair amount of "firefighting" and moving from crisis to crisis?

Here, clarity of roles and expectations is key if you want any chance of succeeding. Have a daily plan, outlining what the top one to three things are that you need to accomplish that day. In developing this daily plan, also try to identify what barriers might stop you from completing these key tasks.

> ### COACH SAYS ...
> *Try to have Plan B ready to use if you get stalled.*

3. Are you very busy, running from task to task and meeting to meeting but not seeing measurable progress?

You let the day, week, or month control you as opposed to your taking charge. You may find that nothing gets done unless you do it. Are you delegating?

> **COACH SAYS ...**
>
> *There are two ways to deal with any event: either control it yourself, or let it control you.*

Look at the skills of your team and fix the problems preventing others from doing the work that you are doing. Is training needed? Whatever it is, fix it. It will stifle all growth in your business. Want to know how to effectively delegate? Skip forward and look at the chapter on leadership. But don't forget to come back.

4. Are you pulled in multiple directions at the same time with little or no time for yourself?

One of the best things you can do is to schedule an actual appointment with yourself. Put it on your calendar and in your Outlook. Set it up as a recurring event on the same day at the same time every week. During this scheduled appointment, work on yourself and a strategic issue that will move your business or your

> **COACH SAYS ...**
>
> *You have to fight for your time as you would for your life. It's that important.*

career one step closer to your goals. You can find out more about how to do this by reading "Put Yourself in Time-Out" on page 121.

5. Do your employees require constant follow-up, doing what they want when they want regardless of what you want them to do?

Make sure your team members understand their roles: why they do what they do and how it fits into what the overall goals are. This applies to everyone from the mailroom to the boardroom. No exceptions. Once they understand their roles, make sure they are proficient in all of their tasks. With that behind you,

> **COACH SAYS ...**
>
> *If your team doesn't know exactly how to win—or even know what winning is—you've lost before the game starts.*

set performance expectations for them and make certain all understand what constitutes satisfactory or better performance. Last but not least, hold everyone accountable to meet or exceed your stated expectations.

6. Do you, today, still have the same passion about what you do as when you first started?

STEP UP: Winning comes one step at a time. Make sure the next step will take you in the right direction.

Look, you have lost your way. It's not unusual. You have gotten so caught up in managing the fires and dealing with clutter and distractions that you no longer know why you do what you do and where it is all taking you. It's like trying to light a fire with damp wood; it flickers and goes out. So first, get away from the day-to-day.

Next, evaluate why you do what you do, namely, your long-term goals. Now re-create your vision so as to define what you want your business or career to look like in three years and how that will satisfy your "why." Then set some goals for the next twelve months, broken down into ninety-day increments, and finally get to work.

PLAY BIG: Identify your biggest distraction. How does it impact (hurt) you? What are the top three steps you can take to eliminate it?

TO STEP UP AND PLAY BIG REQUIRES KNOWING WHAT LEADERSHIP IS AND ISN'T

DON'T STOP LEARNING

This book is keyed to Leadership and other courses found online at Chris Ruisi's Play Big university at www.**StepUpandPlayBig**.com

Great leaders are almost always great simplifiers who can cut through argument, debate, and doubt to offer a solution everybody can understand.

—GENERAL COLIN POWELL

Leadership: Let Me Give it to You as Straight as I Can

If you're like me, you recognize that becoming an effective leader demands hard work and commitment. It requires more than just reading but actual doing and learning from your experiences. Sometimes when we are in the doing mode, we forget some of what we have read and then realize after the

> **COACH SAYS ...**
> *Becoming an effective leader demands continuous hard work and commitment on your part.*

dust settles that there was a different or additional technique that we should have tried.

COACH SAYS ...

*These are the five traits
of good leadership:*

1. *listening*
2. *being in the game 100
   percent of the time*
3. *preparation*
4. *having an open mind*
5. *challenging the team*

At times like this I wish I had a "pocket reminder" so that when I'm confused, I have a simple guide to help me. Having said this, I am not suggesting that there is either a simple or one-size-fits-all approach to leadership. Leadership requires more than just reading but actual doing and learning from your experiences. But, if a simple pocket reminder helps you on your leadership development journey, then so be it.

I looked back over my thirty-five-plus years of corporate experience and realized that in every leadership position I have held, I came up with five traits that, when all else failed, helped get the leadership job done.

Here's how to implement these rules:

Listening

One of the most important standards I set for any team I led was that it was impossible for them to overcommunicate with me. I let my teams know that I hated surprises and that I would let them know when they gave me too much detail. I wanted my team to get into the habit of telling me all that they could. In this way

COACH SAYS ...

*When my team could
see that I was genuinely
interested in what they had
to say, the quality of their
communications improved.*

I could keep my eye on how we were doing on achieving the vision and goals I had set. At this point you might be thinking that my approach was a classic case of TMI (too much info) and micromanaging. Nothing could be further from the truth.

They also knew their roles and where they fit into the big picture, namely, the vision. This also improved the quality and timeliness of their communications to me. As for micromanaging, unless it was absolutely necessary, I never told them what to do. Rather, I asked them to show me how they would do it. Always be listening.

Being in the Game 100 Percent of the Time

> ### COACH SAYS ...
> *If your team sees you as being 100 percent involved, they will act the same way. Be in the game 100 percent of the time.*

Wherever I was, regardless of the topic or situation, I was there 100 percent, or, as some would say, I was "in the present." Nothing would distract me from the task at hand. Some would say, "Come on, Chris! Get real! All leaders have lots on their mind." That's true, but multitasking at the wrong time can be multidumb. Missing one key element in a situation could prove to be a disastrous surprise later on. And guess who would be responsible for it? You! Another reason you want to be in the moment is to set an example. This will improve communications and productivity.

Preparation

This is the simplest of all leadership traits to develop, yet it is the one that most would-be leaders fail to properly address. The ability to prepare is one of the most important habits you can develop, nurture, and maintain. You would be amazed at how simple things become when you take the time to prepare for what needs to be done. Know what you want to achieve in the simplest terms possible, the resources you will need, where and when to get them, what each person's role will be, and so on. This might seem like a lot to do, but if it helps you be successful, isn't preparation a worthwhile investment?

> **COACH SAYS ...**
>
> *Publish an agenda in advance or ask for one to be published that states what will be discussed and what goals are to be achieved.*

For example, one simple way to strengthen your preparation skills deals with how you approach and conduct business meetings. Do you start your meetings by just walking in and trying to wing it? If this is your current approach, you are wasting time, and your productivity is at risk.

Without the necessary preparation you will be doomed to doing things over and over again until you get them right. This approach costs you money, time, and leadership credibility. Be prepared.

Having an Open Mind

I found that I was most effective when I would try to identify other relevant options. It was my job to choose the right option, of course. To do that, I had to keep my mind open to all of the factors involved, some of which I initially might not have been aware of. By keeping an open mind, I was also able to be effective on another key leadership level: staying ahead of other potential problems. By looking at the options, I could see which might cause other issues down the road. This at least gave me a chance to develop a plan to deal with any issues a particular path might generate. Plus, encouraging others to feed me options helped to improve team communications and involvement.

While I knew that keeping an open mind was important, I also knew that at some point I had to make a decision to keep us moving forward. Keeping an open mind to all options does not mean you have to listen to or act on all of them. To do so could paralyze you. I knew that as the leader I had to make things happen. By keeping an open mind, I was better able to consider the most important factors to help me make a decision with incomplete or not-so-perfect data. Keep an open mind, but don't let it paralyze you.

Challenging the Team

The first, and one of the most influential, business mentors I had was a gentleman named George Hoffacker. He had the unique ability, through reflective questions, to challenge me to find the answers on my own. When I was stumped, he challenged me to identify the resources that would help me keep moving forward. To this day I believe that his leadership approach with me—to challenge me to be better—laid the foundation for many of the successes I experienced in my career. He was always there to help me or guide me, but most important, he helped me learn the real measure of my full capabilities. During our discussions, again through reflective questions, he also helped me learn to deal with any obstacles or barriers I might face. He showed me that the solutions to my challenges were well within my grasp.

While he could have easily told me what to do, he knew that approach would shortchange me in terms of my learning and executive development. From my experiences with him, I created one of my own leadership approaches: When my team members wanted to see me about a problem, they had to follow one of two ground rules. Either they had to be able to tell me what they had tried that did not work to solve the challenge, or they had to come in with recommended courses of action they wanted to brainstorm with me before they took action. This approach helped me to help my teams learn how to think about and see their full capabilities, which in turn positively impacted their confidence level and professional growth as well as the growth of the business. No one was allowed to start a sentence with "we have a problem" without ending it with "here's how I think we can solve it." A quote that I recently came across says it best: "Leadership involves inspiring others to be greater than they believe they can be; to help them see how they can exceed their own self-expectations." Challenge your team so that they will grow and help your business grow.

PLAY BIG: Identify one thing you can do over the next six to twelve months to enhance your performance in each of the following areas: listening; being in the game 100 percent of the time; preparation; having an open mind; and challenging your team.

Seven Steps to Make Effective Leadership Simple

Over the course of my corporate career, as well as my career as a leadership keynote speaker, I have had the opportunity to observe, work for, and learn from some great business leaders. I also worked for some—not many, fortunately—who held a leadership position only on an organization chart and had no clue about what it takes to be a real leader. You know the type: a shallow empty suit with a nice smile.

From my experiences with the best leaders I have known, I have compiled what I believe is a list of characteristics that make for an effective leader.

With all of this as background, let's get started on your leadership journey:

1. **Leaders know they are judged not just by what they say but, more importantly, by what they do:** Simply stated, leaders value actions over words. They know that they must lead by example. I hope they know that people—their team, peers, bosses, and even competitors and adversaries—are always watching them. Leaders know that talk is cheap and that the right action at the right time gets things done. As such, in addition to providing direction and instructions, leaders know that they have to act in a way that reflects what they believe in and supports their vision.

2. **Leaders define reality and responsibilities:** You cannot move to a better place without knowing or defining, in the most specific way possible, where you are now. Why? Because the important decisions needed to move forward will be based upon the current reality. Plus, in order for others to see the

value of moving forward, the leader must make certain that he or she understands as clearly as possible the reality of the current situation, that the status quo is no longer viable. With reality accurately defined and understood by all, the leader is then in an excellent position to assign responsibilities to each team member to move the organization forward.

3. **Leaders set performance expectations and hold people accountable to get the job done:** Leaders know that their primary role is to make things happen. To do this they know that the most basic responsibility of every leader is to set expectations. Expectations, when met, make things happen. Yet, many do not make full use of this very valuable tool. Expectations set in motion the steps needed to be taken and the goals needed to be reached in order to make the leader's vision the new reality. People will achieve the expectations set for them only if they are held accountable to do so. I don't mean held accountable in a negative sense, although that is a possibility and sometimes necessary, but rather in a positive, motivational way. People perform best and are the most satisfied when they see themselves making progress as part of a bigger picture.

> ## COACH SAYS ...
>
> *A leader acknowledges team members and helps each of them and the rest of the team see how progress is being made.*

4. **Leaders find ways to challenge their team members to help them grow and stretch their capabilities:** Leaders know that if they get better, their organization will automatically get better. They also know that if an individual team member gets better, the entire team will benefit. Author Rudyard Kipling best described this dynamic of improving the team through the improvement of each individual member when he wrote, "For the strength of the pack is the wolf, and the strength of the wolf is the pack." Each team member, like a wolf, is dependent on the others for his or her collective success. In addition, an effective leader knows that none of his team members, including himself, works to his or her fullest capabilities. He recognizes that as members get better, they begin to tap into and stretch their collective capabilities.

5. **Leaders reward the right actions:** The right actions are those that move the organization closer to the vision that the leader has created. Some will be significant, but most of these actions will be performed daily as part of the usual routine. If the leader has done a good job in defining reality, creating the vision for the future, assigning responsibilities, setting expectations, and holding people accountable, it will be very easy to recognize and reward the right actions.

6. **Leaders never accept below-average performance and act quickly when poor performance has been identified:** Regardless of how good a leader is or how well intentioned he is, the decision to follow him and meet the expectations he has set is a personal one made by each employee. However, just as it is easy to find and reward the right actions, a poorly

performing employee will become painfully obvious. When that occurs, a leader must take quick and decisive action to remedy the situation. This remedy could involve additional training and guidance or more serious actions such as a probationary period or termination. When leaders put off timely action, they run the risk of sending a dangerous message to the better performers on their team, namely, "I will tolerate less than acceptable levels of job performance, so you don't have to work that hard."

7. **Leaders know how important it is to listen to what their team members have to say:** Effective leaders know that one of the best ways to engage their team members is to listen to them when they talk about their job concerns and job challenges, and when they make suggestions for improvements. The team members are on the line, doing the work. They have a valuable perspective to offer, and an effective leader wants to hear what they have to say. Their comments may lead to business improvements that the leader might not otherwise have considered. As I wrote in my blog post, "No trust = No leader," effective listening builds trust. Trust builds or strengthens relationships, and strong relationships are the foundation of a healthy team. Healthy teams are focused and get results. They perform for their leader because they want to, not because they have to.

> ## COACH SAYS ...
>
> *Remember, there's a difference between a leader and a boss. A leader will guide the team to victory. A boss will assign blame for his own failure.*

So, what should you do now? Simple: Conduct your own self-examination to evaluate how well you are leading your team. Ask yourself how well you stack up against the seven points I have listed here. Now is the time for you to take some action on how you can become an even better leader. Remember what I said earlier: when the leader gets better, so does the team, and ultimately the business follows. The one fact you must keep in mind is that you—in fact, all of us—can always be better if we choose to be.

COACH SAYS ...

These are challenging times, and it appears that the challenges will be with us for some time to come. Anne Mulcahy, former CEO of Xerox, said it best when she commented, "There is not a lot of room anymore for senior people to be managers. They have to be leaders."

PLAY BIG:

Of the seven steps identified, pick one and list the top five actions you will take over the next six months to elevate your skills.

TO STEP UP AND PLAY BIG MEANS YOU KNOW HOW TO USE LEADERSHIP

DON'T STOP LEARNING

This book is keyed to Leadership and other courses found online at Chris Ruisi's Play Big university at www.**StepUpandPlayBig**.com

If your actions inspire others to dream more, learn more,
do more, and become more, you are a leader.

—JOHN QUINCY ADAMS

L et's take what we learned about leadership in the previous chapter and put it to use in this one, in which we'll talk about the three laws of leadership and how leaders navigate teams through tough, real-life situations.

Leadership Law Number One: Never Bleed When the Sharks Are in the Water

Finding yourself in a tough and even scary predicament often comes with the territory when you are in a leadership position. During my executive career, I used to describe these situations as being comparable to swimming with a bunch of hungry and unpredictable sharks. I also learned through my experiences that the one thing you never do is bleed when the sharks are in the water with you. Simple, right?

Not quite. In these tough situations, leaders sometimes get bruised and battered, and they bleed. Once the sharks sense that there is blood in the water, the intensity of the crisis accelerates, and the urge to start a feeding frenzy increases. A feeding frenzy in business terms is a complete lack of discipline within the team: They lose their focus. Fear of the unknown becomes the dominating emotion, and the overriding purpose shifts from solving the problem to one of every man for himself. The situation goes from bad to worse, usually at a rapid pace. Right?

Leadership Law Number Two: Use Challenges as Opportunities

It's those episodes of business crisis or chaos that become a defining moment in your professional career. You can't waste any time treading water and hoping that the sharks will get bored and swim away from a free meal. Have you ever walked away once you got a whiff of one of your favorite meals or desserts? I don't think so.

> **COACH SAYS ...**
>
> *Under pressure, leaders are trusted. Bosses are despised. Under pressure, teams want to help their leader succeed. However, they will sit back and watch their boss fail (eaten by the sharks).*

You have to act with purpose while in the midst of the situation. You can't call a time-out or do-over and climb out of the water to assess the crisis. You are in a real-time situation that requires deliberate and committed action, while your team—and everybody else for that matter, including the sharks—is watching your every move, reaction, and step you take. If the leader panics, the team may also sense that there is no path or vision to follow. Confusion and frantic activity become the norm, and the leader may be unable to regain control in a timely and qualitative manner. If, on the other hand, the leader acts boldly and remains calm but vigilant and focused, the team will sense this. Their trust in their leader will grow, and they will follow in an effective way.

Leadership Law Number Three: Always Have a Plan—Always

When sharks start to circle and the game starts to fall apart, the first question a team asks a leader is, "What should we do now?" The *wrong* answer is *always*, "I don't know!" First and foremost, when you find yourself among the sharks, you need a bold plan to help you navigate your way to safety. If you developed a tentative Plan B before the crisis, you are in a good position to figure out your bold solution.

How to Make a Plan

Let's talk about the components of this bold plan. I have followed all of these components during the many chaotic business situations I found myself in. None were the same, but the components of the plan were consistent. I learned something from all of them, and I hope that this learning will be equally valuable to you.

1. **Define and accept reality:** The crisis is there. It will not fix itself, and ignoring it or thinking it will go away by itself will only make it worse (the sharks are getting hungrier).

2. **Engage your team:** Make sure they understand the reality of the situation.

3. **Get it out of your head that you will solve this crisis by yourself:** If you think this, then just sprinkle yourself with seasoning and let the sharks have their way with you. Your team is willing to help you so long as you ask them to. They need to understand the situation better in order for them to step up and play big (www.StepUpandPlayBig.com). There is always strength in numbers.

4. **Make sure you understand the core cause of the crisis:** Knowing how it happened will help you understand how to fix it.

5. **Define the new reality:** This is your vision of what you want it to look like. You know, you get back in the boat or make it land in one piece.

6. **Implement your plan:** Define the roles of your team members and set expectations that everyone understands. Delegation and leadership are key skills.

7. **Communicate with your team:** Give credit when credit is due. During a crisis, emotions run high. Stress and tension will affect your team members' relationships with one another. Move quickly to defuse any team tension. Not only is it distracting, but someone will get bitten, and your plan and you, your team, and your company will fail.

8. **Understand that it may take time to solve the problem:** Try not to declare victory before it has been earned; otherwise

you will find yourself backing over the same ground more times than you need or care to.

9. **Review your plan with your team frequently:** make adjustments, delegate, communicate, and lead.

10. **Don't be afraid of making mistakes:** you will! But learn from them. Focus on always moving forward. Focus on winning.

You will face a crisis in your professional career. Don't run from it. Rather, try to get ahead of it as quickly as you can to get a different perspective on it. As in action/adventure movies, when under attack, people always try to get to higher ground for safety and time to think. Once you have, try the ten steps outlined above.

PLAY BIG: Develop your own shark-repellant kit. What will be the very first step you will take when you find yourself in a crisis? Now develop your second and third steps. Keep going until you are well protected.

No Trust = No Leader

From my own business experiences and in my role as a motivational business speaker, I have learned that one of the most important tools leaders have at their disposal is trust. Without it, they're not leading. They're just going for a walk in the

COACH SAYS ...

The fate of a business can be directly tied to the level of trust the team has in their leader.

park. Think about it: if your team doesn't trust you, why would they follow you or even listen to you? As a professional keynote speaker, I explain that if a leader isn't trusted, a team will not respond to even the simplest request from their leader, let alone the hard ones that require extra effort on their part.

So, if trust is so important, how does a leader go about earning it? That's right, earning it! Too many leadership one-night-stands think that they have earned the trust of their team because of their title. Really dumb, right? But they are not leaders. From my own career experiences and from those of leaders I respect, I have come up with an initial list of things a leader needs to do to earn the trust of his or her team. Here it is:

1. When I am presenting as a leadership keynote speaker, I explain that you need to have a vision of where you want to take your organization. **Effective leaders have a destination in mind** (and then another one after the first one is achieved) and like to get there in the most direct way possible. While there may be some zigging and zagging to deal with obstacles, teams respond best when the leader is confident about the direction in which he or she is going. No vision = No trust.

2. From your vision, **develop a set of clear values that you will adhere to** in executing your strategy to achieve your vision. If you can't place a high premium on things that will describe who you are—your core—and why you do what you do, you are creating a credibility and integrity vacuum in the eyes and minds of your followers. No values (consistently followed) = No trust.

3. Do what you say you will do, or, in other words, **live up to the promises you make**. You've heard the old expression, you can talk the talk but can you walk the walk? Do I really need to explain this further? If you need further explanation, stop now and go do something else. Not walking the walk = No trust.

4. Listen to your employees so that you can build a strong reputation and relationship with them. Hold periodic meetings to keep everyone in the loop. I call them "huddles." Talk one-on-one with them. Ask them about their career goals. I call these EDMs, or employee development meetings. Ask them what is working and what they think can be done to make things better. No listening = No trust.

5. Equally important to your team's development as well as your reputation with them is spending time daily or weekly catching team members doing something right. **Look for every opportunity you can to reinforce the right actions and behaviors** on the part of your team. There is a great book on the subject, titled *Whale Done*, by Ken Blanchard. It's a short but very valuable read. Go get it! No encouragement = No trust.

6. **Get into the habit of admitting your mistakes** when something goes wrong. If your team members see you doing this, they will know that you are human and they will begin to admit, and take responsibility for, their mistakes. Also, when taking responsibility becomes the norm in your business culture, finger-pointing episodes decrease and you

lay the foundation for building a no-excuse culture within your company. Not taking responsibility for your actions = No trust.

7. The example you set through your actions determines how you lead. Hence the concept of leadership by example. As a leader you **set the tone by what you do more than what you say**. This is the single biggest factor in how trustworthy your team believes you to be. As the boss, you need to have a higher level of integrity. The industrialist Andrew Carnegie captured the concept best when he said, "As I grow older, I pay less attention to what men say. I just watch what they do." Not setting the right example = No trust.

8. Finally, to help you earn the trust of your team and boost your team's performance, **learn to take smart risks**. As a professional business speaker, I usually talk about the importance of taking smart risks. I use a turtle in my discussion by asking, "How does a turtle move forward?" I get the usual answers of "one step at a time" or "slowly." The audience usually has an aha moment when I reply that a turtle moves forward by sticking his neck out. The turtle understands all too well that making progress involves, in fact demands, taking risks. There is a lesson here for all who hope to be successful leaders. Once you get comfortable taking risks, coach your team members on how to take them as well. Set the parameters within which they need to stay. Set the performance expectations they must meet and effectively delegate the task. Show them how there are no mistakes in business or in life, only lessons. No risk-taking = No trust.

So, what should you do now? Simple! Conduct a self-examination to evaluate the level of trust you have thus far earned with your team. To help you get started in this effort, let me give you the answer. You can do a better job. Now you take it from here. Create your own plan to get yourself started.

PLAY BIG: Take an honest look at your trust factor. How can you improve it?

What's the one thing you can start doing right now that will convince people you can be trusted? What would you add to the list of things a leader must do to be trusted?

Do You Delegate, or Do You Collect Other People's Problems?

Wikipedia tells us that delegation is the assignment of authority and responsibility to another person to carry out specific activities. However, the person who delegated the work still remains ultimately accountable for the outcome of the delegated work.

Wikipedia goes on to state that delegation, if properly done, is not abdication. Okay, control freaks, now cry out with passion, "Yeah, right!" In general, delegation is good, saving money and time, helping build skills,

COACH SAYS ...

Delegation is supposed to empower a subordinate to make decisions. It is a shift of decision-making authority from a higher organizational level to a lower one. The opposite of effective delegation is micromanagement, in which a manager provides too much input, direction, and review of delegated work.

and motivating people. Poor delegation, on the other hand, will cause frustration and confusion to all of the involved parties. When done poorly, it can be a living hell. Plus, the lousy delegator always blames everyone else.

In his book The One Minute Manager Meets the Monkey, Ken Blanchard talks about the "Four Rules of Monkey Management":

1. **Describe the monkey**: The dialogue must not end until the appropriate "next moves" have been identified.

2. **Assign the monkey**: All monkeys shall be owned and handled at the lowest organizational level consistent with their welfare.

3. **Insure the monkey**: Every monkey leaving your presence on the back of one of your people must be covered by one of two insurance policies:
   a. recommend, then act;
   b. act, then advise.

4. **Check on the monkey**: Proper follow-up means healthier monkeys. Every monkey should have a check-up appointment.

This is probably the best book on delegation that I have found, and at some point in my executive/business coaching client work, I give it to my clients to read. In every case, the lessons in the book hit home with each client. The concept of "insuring the monkey" takes away all of the excuses you control freaks use as to why you cannot (or is it will not?) let go.

One of the dark sides of delegation I had to deal with in my career I labeled as "upward delegation." This happens when a subordinate comes to you and utters these bone-chilling words, "We have a problem" and your (incorrect) response is, "I'll handle it." Sometimes you take it on because you foolishly think it's easier to do it yourself or you don't have time to show the subordinate what to do so you do it. Regardless of what excuse you use—and make no mistake, it is an excuse—the monkey is on your back and you are now a victim—that's right, a victim—of upward delegation, and you did it to yourself.

Over time, I learned to fight and eliminate upward delegation by qualifying my open-door policy by adding two requirements when someone came to tell me, "I need your help," or that all-time favorite, "We have a problem." Remember the rules I mentioned earlier? They were:

- You ask, "Tell me what you tried and why it did not work," or
- you ask, "Tell me what you are thinking of trying, and we'll brainstorm before you take action."

COACH SAYS ...

When your team starts to think, speak and act in this way, they begin to grow, and the growth of your business follows. In addition, you have more time to focus on the things you, as the leader, need to focus on: the strategic issues that will move your business and you forward. This is playing big!

When you, as the leader, lay out performance expectations and stick to them, your team members start to do their homework and are better able to identify, understand, and solve the challenges they confront, in most cases without your help. In essence, they become active participants in finding solutions without having to be told what to do. This simple approach encouraged my team members to think about solutions before they raised the red flag and not to be fearful of either taking action or offering up workable suggestions.

So how do you get started? First and foremost ...

You're going to have to break out of your comfort zone. You're going to have to initially feel comfortable feeling or being uncomfortable, or, as I have often said, "You need to step up and play big." After that, following these simple steps will get you going in the right direction:

1. **Define** the task. Describe clearly what the output needs to be.

2. **Delegate** to a person with proven competence.

3. **Explain** the task clearly, in writing if necessary.

4. **Invite/encourage** questions and feedback.

5. Give a **schedule** and deadline for completion.

6. Periodically **inspect** what you expect.

A warning: The first time you follow this approach, it may not go as smoothly as you might hope. That's okay. Learn from the bumps in the road and apply that knowledge to the next time. Guess what? The next time may not go smoothly either. Just don't quit on this or yourself. Keep working at it. Delegation, done the right way—and you can do it the right way—is hard work. However, it is one of the most effective tools a leader has in his tool kit. So ask yourself, do you really delegate or do you just collect and get swamped by other people's problems? If the answer is that you are a collector, stop right now and change course. Your career, business and quality of life depend on it.

PLAY BIG: It's time to conduct a candid assessment as to whether you are an effective delegator. Write down how you currently delegate work. Be honest. Then, right under it, write down how you know you should delegate. Work on the differences preventing you from being an effective delegator.

See Spot Run:
Effective Leaders Know How to Keep It Simple

Nothing is ever really as hard as it first appears to be. I have often joked that there is something in our genetic makeup that kicks in each morning telling us, "Look for something real easy and then try to make it harder than it needs to be."

COACH SAYS ...

When you don't keep it simple, you damage your ability to build trust with your team and boost their performance.

The fact is that we sometimes tend to make things such as business decisions harder or more complicated than they need to be. Why? Because we do. We overthink the situation and lose sight of the root cause and the best solution. I have found in my real-world experiences that when business leaders do this, they not only hurt their business but their team as well. When working with clients as their executive coach, getting through this barrier can be challenging until they resolve to let go of this damaging habit.

STEP UP:

Want to simplify your life and the life of your team? Here's what you can do:

1. Learn to think, speak and write in simple sentences: noun, verb, and object (don't try to be fancy. It only messes things up).

2. Get all of the input you need to understand the root cause/issue. Get it down on paper.

3. Define what needs to be done. Write it down step by step.

4. Eliminate all of the unnecessary steps. Unnecessary steps make it complicated. For starters, try to eliminate 10 to 20 percent of the initial steps.

5. Understand that to be an effective leader it is okay and necessary to make decisions based on imperfect data.

6. Do it. Measure progress and results.

7. If the desired result is not achieved, don't give up. Make another decision to make it right. Do what is needed to keep moving forward.

8. Stay focused.

We even think that we have to be perfect in our solutions. Let me let you in on a little secret: People who try to be perfect are usually procrastinators. They live in a world of getting ready to get started, to commence to begin. They are always at the starting line, waiting and waiting while others are getting ahead and making progress. We get distracted by thinking about what might happen until we overwhelm ourselves with layers and layers of perceived complexity, confusion, and—here's the big one—*fear*. We eventually confuse others working with us. We let this confusion literally stop us in our tracks.

This last point is something that I cover in detail in many of my talks when I urge audience members to step up and play big.

PLAY BIG: We all like things to be simple. Yet sometimes, by our own actions, we make them complicated. Think about a recent problem or crisis you had to deal with. How could you have handled it in a simpler way? Follow that simple process in the future.

Are You a Real Leader? Take a Lesson from Legendary Baseball Manager Connie Mack.

The best leaders are those who are seen as real: focused on a forward-looking vision; in the present; caring; driven to succeed; appreciative of their team; good listeners; adaptable; trustworthy; and possessing high integrity in all that they say and do (leading by example). Sounds hard? You bet it is, but it is doable.

As I have stated before, effective leaders know that they must make something happen. They excel at directing their team's activity to turn a game plan into something that is not only concrete but measurable. To do this well, they must be able to rally their team and supporters around a series of coordinated actions to get from point A to point B.

One of the best examples of a real leader was the legendary baseball icon Connie Mack. In 1901, he founded the Philadelphia Athletics and managed them for fifty years. During his tenure as their skipper, he collected nine American League pennants and five World Series Championships.

Mack once said, "A big player has to have the will to win. Some players think that this means a constant stream of pep talks during a game directed at other teammates. You can't win a ball game talking about victory; the only way to win is to play to win." You know, step up and play big. And his teams won.

Connie Mack was a real leader in every sense of the word. He rallied his players around the six key points of the culture he wanted to create. He set out his vision, established expectations, and held the members of his teams accountable to meet these standards. He did all of this in a **consistent, persistent and systematic** way. Those of you who know me have heard me use these three words many times before.

There's not much more I can say here other than to challenge you, the reader, to decide if you want to elevate your leadership game. You can and should do this unless you honestly believe that you already are a real leader.

COACH SAYS ...

Learn the lessons taught by Connie Mack. He built the foundation of his achievements on six key points that formed the culture of his team.

- *Always play hard and fair.*

- *Never make excuses.*

- *Be a true sportsman on and off the field.*

- *Always put the team before personal glory.*

- *Be physically and morally sound.*

- *Always judge a player as an individual and never on the basis of his race or religion.*

Do you have values that reflect the culture you want to create? If so, do all around you understand and buy into them completely? If you have not established these values, you need to do so. Take some time right now and establish your own set of rules to live by, live by them, and share them with others.

PLAY BIG: Each of Mack's six points is easily adaptable to your career or business. If you choose to accept this challenge, the first step would be to take out six blank sheets of paper. On the top of each sheet write one of the six points. Under each point write one to three things you can start doing to put that point into practice within your business world.

TO STEP UP AND PLAY BIG REQUIRES NEW OR BETTER HABITS

DON'T STOP LEARNING

This book is keyed to Leadership and other courses found online at Chris Ruisi's Play Big university at www.**StepUpandPlayBig**.com

Motivation is what gets you started. Habit is what keeps you going.

—JIM RYUN, OLYMPIC TRACK STAR

Watching the Game Films

On the path to discovering your real capabilities, you will no doubt experience some obstacles and bumps in the road that may lead to a failure. I believe when that happens, you have the opportunity to recover.

To maximize your capabilities, you must go through recovery from a setback. You must experience it. It's not something you can read about in a book. To leverage your recovery, you must do what I often describe as looking at the game films. Every winning team does it, but the teams that constantly get better do it all the time and ask themselves these four questions based upon the following premise:

If we had to play the game again, based upon what we learned from our experience, what would we

- **start** doing?
- **stop** doing?
- do **more** of?
- do **less** of?

When you encounter a setback or failure, you need to ask yourself these same questions to learn how to elevate your game for the next time. Some people are reluctant to go through this diagnostic exercise because of the pain and fear of reviewing what they did. They would like to put the entire episode behind them forever and run from it as fast as they can. By doing this, they pretty much guarantee that they will make the same mistakes again and never elevate their game to a higher level.

PLAY BIG: Right now commit to using the game film process for every major project or problem you have to deal with. Start with the last one that did not go as well as you had planned. Keep a log of your answers and compare your findings from issue to issue. Your productivity and success rate will improve by using this easy tool.

The Ten Tools Every Leader Must Know How to Use

Let me show you how simple it is to realize and maximize your full capabilities and start building a winning strategy. When you are attempting to build something, you need to know which tools to use and how to use them in the most effective way. So, for our discussion right now, let's look at the tools a leader needs in his or her toolkit.

Tool 1: Confidence: Believe in yourself. You have many gifts, talents, and skills that are waiting for you to use. Many rely on hope, but that means you are waiting for something to happen, and hope is not a strategy. When you have faith in your abilities, you make things happen. The worst that can happen is you make a mistake. Simple! Just fix it. Believe in yourself and not what others tell you about you.

Tool 2: Imagination: If you want to play big, you must first learn to dream big. Many fail to achieve their full capabilities because they set their "success bar" too low. They can achieve more. They just sell themselves short. They expect less from themselves, and eventually others expect less of them. To be big on the outside, you have to be big on the inside. Dream big. See it and go after it. What have you got to lose?

Tool 3: Vision: Take the big dreams and turn them into a very specific vision. Mark Twain once asked, "Why do you look like an envelope without an address on it?" Without a specific vision, you have no address or destination, so what you have inside doesn't matter because you have nowhere to go. Believe in yourself, dream big, and have a big vision that you monitor all of the time.

Tool 4: A plan: Remember what I said about always having a plan? You have one, right? A plan is what makes imagination practical and visions possible. Planning is a key habit. Do it daily.

Tool 5: Movement: This is simple: go to the goal. You have confidence, imagination, and a vision. So take action. Follow the plan. Be in motion. If you don't see opportunity, take action to create opportunity. Action = Results. It's that simple. Just make sure your actions flow directly from your dreams and vision.

Tool 6: Self-discipline: Do what you're supposed to do when you're supposed to do it, even though you don't feel like doing it. Talent without self-discipline is like an octopus on roller skates: lots of motion sideways and backward but no consistent progress forward. Develop the self-discipline habit today. It's big—really big! (There's more about this in the next section.)

Tool 7: Perseverance: Stop using your weaknesses as excuses. If there is something you want to do better or learn to do, get started and don't give up when you stumble and fall. Set improvement targets for each week or month, and within a short time, your weakness and excuses will be gone. Try to manage your life/career with this quote: "Don't accept or offer excuses."

Tool 8: Optimism: When confronted with a crisis, always look for the opportunity. It's there, but you have to find it. But if you give in to defeat, you will never find it and quite possibly develop a quitter's attitude. Also in times of crisis you will find what you are truly capable of.

Tool 9: A good joke: Keep and nurture your sense of humor. Humor is a valuable habit to have. Business is a game and you are supposed to have fun doing it. If you take it too seriously, it will kill you—literally. Think about it, there isn't a mistake you can make that you cannot fix with another decision. When things don't go right, learn from the experience and move on but first take some time to laugh about it. Release the pressure valve now and then with a laugh. You'll be a better business leader for it.

Tool 10: Gratitude: You only get one life. So why not get the most out of it? You work hard, so there should be no guilt associated with enjoying your life. There is some degree of suffering in each of our lives. Don't be a victim of self-induced suffering brought on by all that surrounds you. Make time every day to be grateful for all that you have. Many of us spend too much time obsessing over what others have or what is missing in our lives. If you want more, pursue it.

Never Step Backward

Look, let me be clear. You need to invest in yourself and keep on learning. An executive coach can keep you focused once you decide to move out of your comfort zone. When you decide to stop learning, you become stagnant and all growth comes to a halt. There are some great books out there for you to read. *Think and Grow Rich* by Napoleon Hill, *Eat That Frog* by Brian Tracy, and *Selling the Invisible* by Harry Beckwith are some good ones to start with. But just reading books alone will not do it. Going to as many seminars as you can, especially the cheap ones, will not do it, nor will going to the most expensive ones. You must do more.

STEP UP: What is the "more"? Take the knowledge you collect and put it into practice. That's right. You have to work it. You have to take a risk. You have to make some mistakes and you have to learn how to make glorious recoveries.

You may have heard the expression that "good judgment comes from experience and experience comes from bad judgment." You are the control center of your growth potential. The operative word here is *you*. You are your most valuable asset. Start using *you*. Start using your skills. Start trying new behaviors to see what works best. Start using the stuff in this book. I've often said, "the stuff works, but you have to work the stuff." Bottom line: start playing your game, the game that you were born to play.

PLAY BIG: Go to Chapter 8, titled "Creating Your Own Step Up and Play Big Development Growth Plan." Use the questions supplied and develop your first of many plans.

Self-Discipline or Confusion and Chaos—Your Choice

Self-discipline is the single most important skill/habit after persever-ance that you need to develop to achieve any level of success. It doesn't matter whether you are a business owner, a CEO, or a corporate executive. Self-discipline is a key ingredient to whatever you do.

George Washington said, "Nothing is more harmful to the service than the neglect of discipline, for discipline, more than numbers, gives one army superiority over another."

The best definition of self-discipline, I believe, was written by the famous biologist Thomas Huxley (1825–95). He defined self-discipline as "doing what you are supposed to do, when you are supposed to do it, even though you may not feel like doing it." Self-discipline involves acting on what you know as opposed to how you feel at any given time. As a motivational business speaker, when I talk to my audiences about the critical need to step up and play big, I explain that the absence of strong self-discipline skills is the biggest self-imposed barrier to success that they will ever face.

Stephen R. Covey said, "The undisciplined are slaves to moods, appetites and passions [their emotions]." Have you ever experienced that in your business career?

Self-Discipline is the Cornerstone of Your Ability to Manage Yourself

If you cannot manage yourself, how can you manage—I mean lead—others? Self-discipline is a key component of leadership. Some confuse self-discipline with time management. Those who are confused on this mistakenly think that if they improve their time management skills, they will be in better control of their surround-ings. Well, they have it backward. Let me explain.

If you cannot first manage yourself, how can you manage time? I don't use the term "time management" but rather "you management." **It's all about what you do with the time you have available each day.** If your self-discipline and perseverance skills are lacking, you won't do much with the time you have other than waste it. Wasting time in a leadership role also means that you are delegation challenged. What's the effect of all of this? You, your team, and your business will pay dearly for it.

As you control tasks, you build more self-discipline. As you build more self-discipline, you build more and better "you management" skills. As your "you management" skills grow, your level of self-confidence develops further. And once this

> **COACH SAYS ...**
> *Self-discipline helps you focus on your priorities and control your tasks.*

happens, your self-discipline habit grows stronger preparing you for the next challenge. That's really what life is all about: every time you overcome one challenge, you earn the right to a greater one.

Don't be fooled. Self-discipline is often a very difficult habit to develop and sustain. You need courage to help you push through the barriers you will face in developing your self-discipline skill.

STEP UP:
Let's talk about how you can develop and strengthen your self-discipline skill set:

Focus on when you should start a task as opposed to when you need to complete it. When you focus on the completion date first, you leave yourself open to procrastination and missed deadlines as well as missed opportunities. How many times have you said, "I'll get to it later"? Be honest.

Start to *plan* each day the day before. Make your next-day plan the last thing you do before you go home. A daily plan helps give a clearer picture of what needs to be done that day. The clearer the picture, the more likely you will hit your goals for that day.

Have *goals,* realistic and achievable ones. Why? Goals help you map out your journey. They establish important mile markers. Goals are one of the key ingredients that help us build the resilience and courage to stay focused on what is possible.

When creating your daily plan, ask yourself **two questions:** First, what is the one thing I must get done today? Second, what could stand in the way of my getting this key task done? By knowing your key task, you have more clarity. Thinking about what obstacle you might face will give you time to figure out a solution to it, or, at minimum, a way around it. In addition, this process helps you to "own your goal."

Start to take on those tasks or challenges that in the past you would have avoided until the last minute or just completely ignored. These are the challenges that are within your level of ability but represent a *stretch* of your limits. I don't want you to completely leave your comfort zone but rather start to stretch it. This is where your courage will come in to play. Rest assured, when you "stretch it" regularly, it will get bigger, and that's good news for you and any future success you plan to achieve.

In addition to these comfort-zone stretchers, start to **tackle** those things that you put off because you just don't feel like doing them or just don't like to do them. Okay, let's be honest. Maybe you put things off because you are lazy. Ouch! That might have hurt.

It will require **hard work and focus.**

Above all, you must **be persistent** and not give up when you experience some failures or setbacks as you begin to stretch and strengthen your self-discipline skill set. The consequences of giving up are too serious professionally and personally.

No wonder some equate self-discipline with mental toughness. Vince Lombardi said, "Mental toughness is many things and rather difficult to explain. Its qualities are sacrifice and self-denial. Most importantly, it is combined with a perfectly disciplined will that refuses to give in. It's a state of mind; you could call it character in action."

Developing and enhancing your level of self-discipline demands that you accept the fact that it will require courage, hard work, willpower, focus, and persistence. But the rewards of being in control of your circumstances and destiny far outweigh the sacrifice. Or, do you like being a victim and enjoy the chaos and feelings of being constantly confused and overwhelmed that come with it?

PLAY BIG: Start developing your goals for the day. Be realistic and don't overcommit. Identify the top one or two things that you must do that day. Try to identify what will get in your way and how you will deal with the distraction. Take baby steps for starters but do it every day, the same way, day after day.

Perseverance Means Never Giving Up

The entrepreneur Estee Lauder said, "When I thought I couldn't go on, I forced myself to keep going. My success is based on persistence, not luck."

Perseverance means never quitting. As a leadership keynote speaker, I try to make this point as many times as I can to my audiences when I talk about these critical success principles. There are many true stories about people who have demonstrated this trait including Thomas Edison who invented the light bulb and Lance Armstrong who fought cancer and went on to win the Tour de France seven consecutive times. The fact is that they would not allow themselves to give up. They, by their actions, demonstrated that they knew how to step up and play big, and not giving up has to be practiced and developed into a habit. In addition, the concept of perseverance and never giving up often surfaces when I work with my coaching clients, guiding them through the many challenges they face.

We all have a dream or a goal that we would like to accomplish. Oftentimes the difference between accomplishing the goal and not doing so is the strength of your belief in yourself that you will overcome obstacles. Have you ever thought about why some people never reach their personal or business goals? Sometimes there are good reasons that are beyond their control, but often it is because they lacked perseverance. The fact is that very few people get it right the first time, or even the second or third time. The difference is that they learn from their mistakes and adjust their approach going forward. In other words, they don't give up. They live with the belief that in life there are no mistakes, just a variety of learning experiences.

Some of the challenges you will face in life or in business will be very hard. However, when they are confronted head-on, they offer the opportunity to strengthen your perseverance habit.

> ## COACH SAYS ...
> *It is always easier to give up, and by doing so, it becomes even easier to quit the next time you have to face another challenge.*

Vince Lombardi said, "Once you learn to quit, it becomes a habit." Once you get into the habit of giving up, you start to set lower expectations for yourself, which can be deadly to your career or business. When this happens, other people also begin to expect less from you and opportunities pass you by. The end result is, by giving up, you have started to sabotage yourself. Your success is no longer in your control. Warning! At this point, start getting used to being a victim as opposed to a master of your circumstances. As a motivational business speaker, I spend a great deal of time talking to audiences about the importance of avoiding self-sabotage.

You must decide early on that regardless of what happens, you must never give up. Each time you successfully work through an obstacle, barrier or setback, you become stronger, better, and more resilient. You gain more self-confidence in your ability to handle the new challenges and obstacles that wait on the road ahead.

Yogi Berra said, "It ain't over till it's over." The lesson that Yogi was giving us is simple: never assume anything is really finished or officially over until it's really finished or officially over. When you think you are beat, remember Yogi's message. He went on to say this: "Be calm, be patient, and don't overworry. Good things can happen if you persevere."

PLAY BIG: Think about the last time you gave up too early on a goal. Looking back, what could you have done differently? Whenever you are faced with the possibility of giving up, stop and take a deep breath—ice cream usually works for me—and then see what you could do instead to keep moving forward.

Road Kill—Pay Attention! Bad Things Can Happen Fast on the Road

A while ago I read a great book by Andrew Sherman, titled *Road Rules*. It goes into detail about twelve essential rules for navigating the road of life. Chapter 1 is titled "Be the Truck and Not the Squirrel." It outlines the reasons that squirrels end up as road kill.

The book reports that more than 42 million squirrels meet their demise every year on roads in the USA. So what causes the squirrels' demise? Three things really: First, they were killed by something stronger and faster than they were. Second, they didn't see it coming. Third, their lack of action at a very critical and dangerous moment did them in. The question becomes: In your professional career do you exhibit in any way the traits that caused the squirrels' demise?

Chapter 1 also describes three basic facts: First, "trucks are durable, strong … and build on their momentum as they move closer to their destination (goal)." The second basic fact is that "squirrels are generally happy to eat acorns and mind their own business until one day they end up in the wrong place at the wrong time and WHAM." The rest is, sad to say, history. The third fact is that "in today's unpredictable world and economy, it's more important than ever to position yourself to be the truck."

In much of my public speaking, I talk about what people do to set low expectations for themselves, work below their full capabilities, and self-sabotage their careers or business. In essence, they set themselves up to become the business equivalent of road kill. These self-made victims lack planning skills. They do not know how to set priorities or take timely and critical action. They clearly have no self-discipline, and they have no idea how to set goals or follow them.

So, what should you do? First, go buy the book. Next, read it. Finally, try to put to use its valuable information to change where

you might be standing on the road of business—or life—or else …
well, you know: you might become road kill!

PLAY BIG: Are you properly positioned to leverage your strengths to give you an edge, flexibility, and momentum? Start to plan. Set priorities and goals to always give yourself the advantage. What's the one thing that could cause you to be road kill? What's the one thing you can and should do to avoid it?

Show Me a Man or Woman Who Excels at Putting Out Fires …

Lots of people pride themselves on being experts in dealing with a crisis or being able to put out fires. The question is **how many of these fires do they actually create** because of a lack of a clear and specific vision, goals, and planning? They put out the fire that they started, but how much damage do they cause and leave behind for others to clean up? Show me a man or woman who excels at putting out fires, and I will show you a pyromaniac.

I have also found in my coaching experience that these folks usually settle for below-average results because they are more focused on putting out their self-created fire than on the impact it has on what they are trying to accomplish or the people they work with. Make no mistake. Pyromaniacs have a devastating effect on their employees.

So, what causes this? Well, a couple of things. First, they lack a clear and specific vision. They have no idea where they want to go or how they will get there. Look, it isn't always clear how to run a business or serve in a senior executive role. But trying to be successful in a making-it-up-as-you-go mode has very significant challenges, many of which could be avoided with a vision. Your vision is your dream for the future. A business without a vision is directionless. It lacks purpose and heart. It lacks the essential idea from which commitment, growth, and a sense of personal achievement emerge. Without a vision, you are well positioned to create fires.

The next cause of business fires is a lack of clear and specific goals—Yup! Goals, specific stuff, not the well-intentioned thoughts or things you will get around to doing when you resolve some of the other self-made crises in your life. Constantly think about and focus on your vision and goals, as they will help drive you and sustain you during the crazy times—you know, those times when you would otherwise easily start a fire!

> **COACH SAYS ...**
>
> *A vision is a clearly articulated, results-oriented picture of a future you intend to create. It is a dream with direction.*

STEP UP:

Based on your vision, write down specific, clear, and time-sensitive goals which you have a committed desire to achieve.

Last but not least is a lack of clear and specific planning. To avoid being a fire-starter, you should establish a simple plan that lays out the initial three to five steps you need to take toward your top three goals. Focus on those goals and take meaningful, daily action on the initial steps to build momentum toward achieving them. Your plan should break down the steps into daily activities. Your plan should accurately reflect the time you will need to work on your tasks. There is a famous quote that sums it up best: "If you fail to plan, you plan to fail." The choice is yours.

PLAY BIG: Start to do the following: At the end of each day, plan your next day. Be realistic in creating your daily plan. Think in terms of tasks or to-do's and always plan out your next three to five steps, as in a chess game, to achieve a specific goal. To avoid unpleasant surprises, try to think about what could go wrong and how you would deal with it to stay on course. Always know what your worst case, best case, and most realistic case scenario will be.

Some Brilliance from Yogi Berra:
What Did He Say About That Fork in the Road?

You are at a critical crossroads, and you can't stand there too long trying to determine which way to go. The choices are clear. One is to accept the status quo, curl up into a complacent ball, and accept the fact that you will forever be a victim of the circumstances you created. That's right—you created! The other choice is to change the status quo, create a new reality, and start down that road to becoming a master of the circumstances and opportunities that you create. That's right—you create!

"When you come to a fork in the road, take it," Yogi Berra said.

Here's what Yogi meant by this brilliant bit of advice. According to Yogi in his book with the same title as his quote, "People are always afraid of making the wrong choice. But no matter what decision you make ... you shouldn't look back. Trust your instincts." Yogi went on to say, "Make a firm decision. Make sure it feels right … don't second-guess yourself. But on big life decisions, get advice if you can."

Bottom line: Accept responsibility for your business/career and life. If you don't like where you are, do something about it—now. Determine where you want to be, create your plan, take action, and implement it one step at a time.

PLAY BIG: To improve your decision-making skills, always consider the worst possible outcome and whether or not you can live with it. If you can, then decide. If you cannot, seek some advice. Never get caught trying to study all of the sides of a circle as part of your decision-making process. The goal is always to keep moving forward.

Never Chase a Skunk

During my thirty-plus years in the corporate world, one of the most valuable lessons I learned was: "Never chase a skunk because the skunk has fun and you get smelly."

Now, this will not be that difficult to follow. It's actually very simple. I guarantee that after you read this, your first reaction will be to recall all of the times in the past when you got tricked, fooled, or sucked into chasing the skunk. The next reaction I want you to have is to be more alert when you encounter a "skunk," and, no matter how hard the skunk tries, you resist being lured into chasing him. If you can master this habit—and there is no reason why you shouldn't. Let me repeat: there is no reason why you shouldn't—you will have learned a very important time (you) management lesson. You will be less frustrated and angry—everybody around you, pets included, will like this—and you will be a better a leader. So here goes—a very simple explanation:

The Skunk: a thick-headed, very opinionated, and usually wrong person who attempts to engage you in what he calls an "intellectual" discussion, or—the approach I like best—says, "I would like to get your opinion on something." I describe this type of person as "an answer in search of a question." He has this uncontrollable need to be heard. You know who he is. You've met him, and I know you have fallen for the "chase."

The Chase: really simple. You engage in the "intellectual" discussion. Here's the worst part: you got into this discussion knowing it was wrong. Right? Admit it! And you are wasting valuable time.

The Fun (for the skunk): it doesn't matter how dumb the skunk may be, he is in fun heaven because, by engaging him, you validated every aspect of his position, and now you think you can win. Even if you are right and punch holes in every aspect of the skunk's position, he is dumb to begin with and will never concede a point.

You get smelly: those watching you get "sprayed" with the skunk's "intellectual" scent will be wondering why you ever got involved and might wonder whether you are more like the skunk.

The box on this page has three simple steps every skunk chaser needs to know. If you can follow those three steps, here's what you will learn:

First, **time management:** This should be obvious. You will not waste any time in this effort and can concentrate on something more important.

Second, **frustration and anger levels will go down,** and you will be a better person for it. Everyone around you will notice it and be thankful. Trust me. They will.

Third, **leadership**—leading by example: One of the points I make in my executive coaching activities is that others will notice how you handled this and will want to pay more attention to someone who knows how to work through the clutter and focus on what's really important.

> # COACH SAYS ...
>
> *Attention all skunk-chasers! Do you know what you're doing? If you're closing in on a skunk, you'd better have a plan.*
>
> • *First, know when you are confronted with a skunk. The markings are very visible.*
>
> • *Next, be polite but don't fall for the chase, especially if it's not that important.*
>
> • *Finally, remember these lyrics from the classic Dionne Warwick song: "Walk on by."*

The next time you are faced with the decision to "chase a skunk" in an argument or discussion, ask yourself, "**Is it really that important?**" In most cases it isn't, and you have avoided a conflict and a waste of your time. You do have better things to do. Right?

Think about it.

PLAY BIG: Learn to develop patience when faced with the urge to "chase a skunk." Being impulsive generally will distract you. Think about developing a standard response or course of action when faced with this type of distraction. Maybe just a simple response, such as "that's interesting," and turning and walking away will work. Try it. In almost every instance, it's not that important, and you definitely do have better things to do.

Never Believe Your Press Release

A while ago, we read how the former Hewlett-Packard (HP) CEO, Mark Hurd, lost his job over "expense report irregularities." While I will not question, at this time, the decision of HP's board to ask Mr. Hurd to resign, I do want to examine how Mr. Hurd put himself in this position in the first place.

When I was promoted to senior executive vice president and a member of the office of the chairman at USLIFE (NYSE), the ink was not yet dry on the press release about me when I got my first in-your-face lesson in leadership and good judgment from my best friend, Tim Sullivan. Tim was our CFO and a big man, physically (6'-6") and in his loyalty to me and USLIFE. Tim walked into my office, closed the door, picked me up, pinned me to the wall, and said, "Congratulations on your promotion, but don't ever believe your press release and do something stupid! You're our leader and we are all depending on you."

What Tim was telling me was that my actions, right or wrong, would affect not only our business but also the careers and lives of the employees who made up my team. Tim was saying, "You need to be our coach, our mentor, and our leader."

At that moment I realized that if I were going to be successful in boosting profitability and company results, I needed a team who would trust me, and I had to earn that trust every day. I always knew that but now understood the critical importance of putting my beliefs into consistent actions, and I also learned that if you take care of your team, your team will take care of you and perform for you as well.

A press release is an announcement to the media of an event, performance, or other newsworthy item. If it is about a promotion or other good news, the goal is to create buzz and paint the best picture possible. Sometimes certain issues are expanded upon a bit beyond reality to get the readers' attention.

Many former business leaders believed their press releases and concluded that they were above it all and could take certain liberties without question:

- Mr. Hurd at HP described certain expenses he incurred.
- Dennis Kozlowski of Tyco, who thought nothing of spending $6,000 for a shower curtain, is currently a resident at a government-run facility.
- Former Bear Stearns CEO Jim Cayne reportedly played bridge while the company collapsed.

I have found that when you are in a leadership position in either the corporate world or in a small to midsized business, you have to act like a leader besides being called one. You need to hold yourself to higher expectations or standards than the ones you expect your team to meet. Why? Because **the most important tool a leader has is the trust and respect he earns** from his team. A leader develops his trust tool through actions and deeds as well as through words. The smallest indiscretion can be devastating to his or her ability to lead.

STEP UP: Make sure you take only what you deserve and have earned.

Some misguided so-called leaders think that because of their lofty status or title they are entitled to extras. Nothing can be further from the truth or reality. This type of thinking and, unfortunately, actions damage careers, the employer, and the trust followers place in their leaders.

The only thing worse than believing your press release is to write your own press release and then believe it. I know a CEO of a technology company who has fallen into this trap. He introduces himself by quoting his self-written press release. The only thing he doesn't have yet is his own theme music. Check back with me later to see if he does and also composes it himself.

I really can't stress enough the dangers of an entitled outlook. That's

> **COACH SAYS ...**
>
> *When you think you are entitled to extras, you get into trouble.*

what Tim was telling me in the best way he could, directly and in my face. I am forever grateful for his lesson. It is one of the concepts that have become the basis of my executive coaching approach.

PLAY BIG:

Stay grounded. Understand the full scope and limits of your role. Write both down, the scope and the limits. Keep the notation handy. Give a copy to a trusted advisor and ask him or her to remind you when you exceed either. Next, make a list of all of things you are grateful for. Keep it in your pocket at all times and review when you feel tempted to do something that can only be described as colossally stupid.

Wishing and Hoping Amount to Putting Your Head in the Sand

When facing a crisis, many just try to get though it with the least amount of damage or personal involvement as possible. They are willing to be a victim as opposed to a master of their circumstances. They put their heads in the sand and get their competitive/market share "butt" kicked.

Some hunker down and hope that it will pass and everything returns to normal. As they bury themselves deep in their bunker, others step up to the challenge, look for the opportunities, play big … and emerge as the winners. Some go right into a defensive mode while others choose to take a more offensive stance.

The greatest opportunity belongs to those who use a challenge, crisis, or chaos to improve their business and themselves. They know how to keep their heads up in a crisis. They know that you must constantly stay focused on winning in order to win.

A Clear Vision of What You are Trying to Accomplish Helps in a Crisis.

Without a vision, you are like a ship in an angry ocean with no rudder: you are at the mercy of the wind, waves, and currents. A vision helps you see the opportunities in a crisis as your way forward.

A vision also feeds your passion and helps you use that passion to push through the crisis.

Stop wishing and hoping. Stop hunkering down and putting your head in the sand and waiting for the storm to pass and for things to get back to "normal."

> **COACH SAYS ...**
>
> *While you're hiding, a new normal is taking shape, and you may miss the opportunities that come with it.*

PLAY BIG: Don't get caught up in the emotion and fear that comes with a crisis. Determine what you must do to gain control of the situation. Running or hiding from it only makes it worse.

Playing It Too Safe

Once you get into the habit of playing it safe, you next begin to use, with increasing frequency, the most deadly and dangerous four-letter word in our daily vocabulary: *can't.* You talk yourself into validating all of the things you believe you "can't" do.

> **COACH SAYS ...**
>
> *When you play it too safe, you sabotage yourself, your dreams, and your goals.*

When you reach this point, alarms and warnings should be sounding. You are actually shrinking your capabilities. Eventually others will agree with your self-imposed limitations and will expect less from you also, and, by the way, you will easily meet those lower expectations they have set for you.

Doing just enough to get by actually holds you back from using your full capabilities. You get used to living beneath your dreams. Why would you want to do that?

STEP UP: **RISK AND REWARD:** Many people would be surprised to learn that it really doesn't take a lot of additional effort to be better than average. If you don't experience a setback now and then, you are playing too safe.

Over the years, I have coached or mentored hundreds of executives and business leaders to eliminate the devastating effects of *can't*. When they said to me, "I can't," my initial response was always, "Why not?" The discussion that followed generally led to discovering how the individual could stretch his or her capabilities but only if he or she were committed to doing the work to get to that place.

Consider this: Jimmy Johnson, the legendary coach who led the Dallas Cowboys to two consecutive Super Bowl Championships, once said, "Do you want to be safe and good, or do you want to take a chance and be great?"

PLAY BIG: Don't let the fear of making a mistake hold you back. Every time you make a mistake, write down what happened and what you learned from it. Keep a diary of this information and review it as needed. Apply what you learned from each mistake to some future opportunity.

You Are What You Think—Really!

Many others have written about the importance of recognizing that you are what you think. I have read two excellent books that cover this subject in a detailed but easy-to-follow way. One book is *The Magic of Thinking Big* by David J. Schwartz, PhD., and the other—my favorite—*Think and Grow Rich* by Napoleon Hill. Because both of these books, and probably many others, have covered this topic better than I can, I decided to include my favorite passage from *Think and Grow Rich* as my small contribution to this key aspect of personal success. Enjoy.

If you think that you are beaten, you are.
If you think you dare not, you don't.
If you like to win, but you think you can't,
It is almost certain you won't.

If you think you'll lose, you are lost,
For out in the world we find,
Success begins with a fellow's will.
It's all in the state of mind.

If you think you are outclassed, you are.
You've got to think high to rise.
You've got to be sure of yourself before
You can ever win a prize.

Life's battles don't always go
To the stronger or faster man.
But sooner or later the man who wins
Is the man WHO THINKS HE CAN.

Believe in yourself and your abilities. There is nothing wrong with regular positive "self-talk" to keep the right, positive mental perspective. If you don't do it, nobody else will. Enough said.

PLAY BIG: First, get into the habit of reading this verse several times each week. Next get into the habit of using affirmations on a daily basis to fill your mind with positive "self-talk." Convince yourself that there is no choice other than to achieve success.

TO STEP UP AND PLAY BIG MEANS HANDLING THE TOUGH STUFF

DON'T STOP LEARNING

This book is keyed to Leadership and other courses found online at Chris Ruisi's Play Big university at www.**StepUpandPlayBig**.com

Tough times don't last. Tough people do.

—GREGORY PECK

Making Tough Decisions: How to Cut the Tail off a Dog

Now before you all get mad at me, I am not a supporter of any form of animal cruelty. In fact, Riley Rose, our golden retriever is under my desk having a grand old time with a chewy toy while Toby, our Westie, is also under my desk waiting to take that chewy toy away from Riley as soon as she looks the other way. So I use my title/story to help to get a very important point across.

Some often delay making tough and important/critical decisions on a timely basis because they fear the outcome. So, to avoid this "perceived" result, we either make a series of small and less effective decisions, or we take no action, hoping the matter will take care of itself. When we do this, we actually do more harm because we are prolonging a bad situation and in many cases making it worse. This approach can be a fatal error for a business leader or business owner whose success sometimes depends on whether he can make tough decisions in a timely fashion, based on not-so-perfect information.

There was an old saying that my former boss would use when we faced an important and usually tough unpopular decision: "When you have to cut the tail off a dog, you go right to the butt [he used the three-letter version of the dog's anatomy] and cut it off." If you try to cut it off a piece at a time (little, less effective decisions) all you are doing is making that dog angry (making the problem worse), and every time he sees you coming at him with scissors, he's going to get angrier. One day that dog is going to strike back at a time when you least expect it. The problem, as bad as it first was, is now worse and bordering on a crisis.

> **COACH SAYS ...**
>
> *Get tough decisions behind you so you can focus on moving forward.*

So, when you have a tough decision to make, understand the outcome you want to achieve and take deliberate and focused action. Get it done and get it behind you.

STEP UP: Here are six proven steps you can follow when a problem or chaos causes you to make a tough/important/unpopular decision:

1. **Break** the problem down into smaller pieces.

2. **Determine** the desired outcome.

3. Identify the **obstacles.**

4. Determine one to three **choices of action.**

5. **Pick** the best way forward.

6. Decide and do it—**don't look back.**

It sometimes takes bold action to achieve bold results and earn the trust and respect of those around you.

PLAY BIG: Commit to yourself to follow those six steps to effectively make tough decisions on a timely basis. Think about a past situation in which you hesitated. How could these six steps, if used properly, have resulted in a better outcome?

It's Not My Fault! Oh, Really?
Then Stop Making Excuses!

Business expert Jim Rohn once said, "You must take personal responsibility. You cannot change the circumstances, the seasons, or the wind, but you can change yourself."

Albert Ellis, an American psychologist who, in 1955, developed rational emotive behavior therapy, once said, "The best years of your life are the ones in which you decide your problems are your own. You do not blame them on your mother, the ecology, or the president. You realize that you control your own destiny."

Each of us, at one time or another, has made an excuse about a deadline we missed, work we didn't do, or some other task that fell short of what we promised. Some of us are so good at making excuses that it happens almost automatically or unconsciously as we attempt to avoid any responsibility for why something went wrong.

Maybe we do it because we don't want to get in trouble or we don't want to look bad in front of our coworkers, friends, family, boss, or pet. We just don't want anyone to think less of us. I guess it's a misguided part of our emotional and

> ## COACH SAYS ...
> *From my perspective, there is no such thing as a good excuse.*

psychological approach to defending or protecting ourselves. We even go as far as to justify our excuse when we say, "But I have a good excuse."

All excuses are bad. An excuse means that, for whatever reason, you have made the decision to not step up and take ownership or responsibility for your actions or lack thereof. You are in essence saying, "It isn't my fault. Don't hold me accountable." Well, that's just old fashioned you-know-what.

It's amazing and scary just how much effort people put into coming up with what they think is a good excuse. If they directed half of that effort into doing the right thing, there would be no cause for alarm. One of the reasons, I think, people make an excuse is that they fear making a mistake. I read once that the greatest mistake you

Bench Injuries

But what really happens when you get into the habit of making excuses?

- First, the very people from whom you are trying to gain sympathy and understanding begin to see you as someone who just cannot be depended upon. They know that you always have a reason—oops! I mean excuse—why something didn't get done.

- Next, you are seen as being lazy and defensive.

- Your constant self-victimization becomes old, and eventually others will not want to be around you. In fact, the only people you will attract are other self-made victims, namely, other excuse makers.

- You become so good at making excuses that your reality becomes twisted and you start to identify why you can't do something even before you fully understand what needs to be done.

- Finally, your life becomes an ever-increasing circle of lost personal and professional growth and opportunities.

can make in life is to be continually fearful that you will make one. An excuse becomes their misguided attempt to get others to sympathize with them and cut them a break. They are trying to position themselves as the victim and not the cause.

Some of the most important keys to your success are not your technical knowledge or how you apply it to your role. Rather, your perseverance to see something through to a successful end, your no-fear attitude toward failure, and your commitment to learn from your mistakes will help you develop the level of responsibility and maturity needed to make you a no-excuse player.

The best way that I know how to move in this direction is captured in the phrase, "Fake it till you make it." Now, I am not suggesting that you be dishonest or deliberately mislead others. Rather, to me this approach means that you are willing to try something, and in the process take a reasonable risk and that you have faith and confidence in your abilities to essentially learn on the job. You view any mistakes you might make as "learning opportunities."

The next time you are faced with the choice of offering an excuse or stepping up and taking responsibility and ownership for your actions, take a time-out before you act. Consider for a minute if you are willing to put your courage, confidence, self-respect, and reputation at risk. Remember that others will judge you based on your actions. Do you want to be seen as the person who has the courage to take responsibility for his or her actions or the person who always has an excuse? Choose wisely.

PLAY BIG: Decide to build a no-excuse culture around you. Take 100 percent responsibility for your actions. Write down five bad things that happen to you or others when you make an excuse. Keep this list on your desk.

Fire Yourself!

That's right, I said, "Fire yourself!" This act alone will probably be the best and most important thing you can do for your business or your career right now.

In the process of firing yourself, make sure you do an in-depth exit interview so that you understand completely the reasons for this harsh and necessary action.

Oh! Don't forget to throw yourself a going-away party and buy yourself a gift—not too expensive. You will want to take this occasion—the party—to tell the boss (you) exactly what you think about him and what you would do if you were in charge. And, when you've done all of these things, figure out what you need to do and who you have to be to rehire yourself so you can become the "right" person in charge.

At times, business owners and leaders become so caught up in their own strategies and methods that they have great difficulty breaking free or letting go of what they have become very comfortable doing. They are so heavily invested in their my-way-or-the-highway approach that they have become oblivious to the fact that the world has changed around them and it is time to do some things differently, or begin a dangerous downward spiral from which there may be no recovery.

> ## COACH SAYS ...
>
> *All of us at some point in our careers were new somewhere. Back then it was easy to take a fresh perspective and challenge other people's assumptions or thinking. It's always easier and more comfortable to criticize someone else's thinking as opposed to stepping back and taking a hard look at your own actions and ideas.*

I read recently that Jack Welch, General Electric's legendary chairman, would meet at the beginning of each year with his senior staff and instruct them to act as if they were brand new in their roles. During this process he would ask them to act as if they had no preconceived notions or prejudices and look afresh at their roles and the business.

The approach that Welch followed is very similar to what I ask my clients to do when we work on "watching the game films." Simply stated, watching the game films requires that you use your experiences to freshen or renew your perspective. If done properly, you learn what you would do differently to prepare for the future. To leverage your knowledge you have to be brutally honest with yourself, questioning the status quo and letting go of those assumptions that are no longer valid. This exercise is not for the timid, and excuses are strictly forbidden. The goal is to learn and not to justify your past actions. It may be painful to your ego, but the stakes and rewards can be extremely high.

But let's get back to firing yourself. If you have done the game films exercise properly, you should have a better insight into what has or has not worked for you in the past and what needs to be done in the future.

STEP UP: Here's where you need to tell the boss—that's you—what needs to be done.

What areas or skills does the boss need to enhance or even develop to be able to lead more effectively—leadership, delegation, better communications, and so on?

1. What things should the boss—still you—stop doing or do differently going forward? Could goal setting or having a clear business vision work here? Maybe better communications? Remember, the goal is to bring a fresh perspective to how you do what you do.

2. With the completion of this candid self-assessment, you now have to ask yourself, "What do I need to do to rehire myself?" This is where a detailed game plan for your enhanced performance comes into the picture. The game plan should be specific and goal-oriented.

Now it's time to rehire yourself. Consider what you need to do to prepare yourself to reapply for the job. What contributions or skills would you bring to the table to make a real and measurable difference?

In this process, be sure that you can answer this question: Are you the type of leader you would work for? If you cannot work for you, why would anyone else? It's important that you create a work climate in which others will want to work for and with you. Employees want to be led, not managed. They are looking for someone to make them feel that they are making an important contribution. Are you that person? You must know the answer. If it's no, fix it.

People also want to work for a leader who holds himself to the same high standards to which he holds his team. In other words, are you a leader in words and deeds or just words?

So, you have before you a tremendous opportunity to assess yourself, refresh your perspective and think about what you would do if you had the chance to start over. But you need to act boldly to reshape not only your business but also yourself and your future. You need to step up and play big—no excuses, just focused action. It's your future, what do you want to do about it?

PLAY BIG: Understand the importance of being committed to ongoing learning and self-improvement. Create an annual self-improvement plan or goal for yourself. Be sure to monitor your progress on a quarterly basis. Find a mentor and ask for his or her input on your plan and to hold you to it.

Do You Have What It Takes to Be the Boss?

He was called the Boss out of respect because everyone recognized that he was a born leader. He was driven to succeed. People had one of two reactions to him: they either liked him or disliked him.

There was no middle ground. Say what you want, even if you disliked him and disagreed with his approach, one thing was always perfectly clear: you always knew where he stood on an issue. This is key for any effective leader.

He was George Steinbrenner.

To describe his management style as unique and colorful would be an understatement. His style worked for him. It may not work for you. Regardless, every boss has a unique style. Some styles work and some don't. However, Steinbrenner did get results—and made many players very wealthy in the process—by winning eleven pennants and seven championships after he bought the Yankees in 1973. At the end of the day, business results do matter.

Not everyone wants to be a boss or should be a boss. There is no shame in being the best you can be at what you feel you do best. However, if you do aspire to be a business leader, the title alone will not make it happen, nor will waiting for the leadership genie to appear and sprinkle you with leadership dust. So, if you have decided to be a leader, what are you doing to find your style, develop it, and make it work for you and your team?

Steve Tobak, a popular blogger and partner at Invisor Consulting, in one of his blog posts described the key aspects of Steinbrenner's management style. I have summarized some of them as follows:

1. He made sure his players knew who the Boss was.

2. He was demanding. He said that he learned from his father that "I can't" was never an acceptable answer.

3. He hired the best and kept them.

4. Failure was never an option. He paid the best and expected his team to win.

5. He had a singular focus: **win**. He once said, "Winning is the most important thing in my life, after breathing. Breathing first, winning next."

6. He instilled that winning focus within his organization.

Let's review some of these in a bit more detail and draw some comparisons to you, your business, and your professional growth.

First, earn your title: If you don't have a vision for your company, your team, and so on, you are not a leader and clearly will never be. Duh? Think about it. If you have no vision of where you want to go, how do people know when, how, where, and why to follow you? Don't think for a second that Steinbrenner built his shipping business or the Yankees by making it up as he went. He had a plan, a vision that he constantly adjusted as he collected more knowledge and experience. He learned from the good times as well as the bad times. That's what leaders do: they learn and apply that knowledge to their present situation to create the future they want and boost their companies' performance.

Second, know where you're going: With a vision, leaders are able—or better be if they expect to keep their job—to set expectations and standards for the team. Steinbrenner set high standards for his team and held them to these expectations. On this point alone he was most consistent. For you leader-

COACH SAYS ...

Throughout my career, I was always in a leadership position. The following information developed from my successes and my mistakes. In all honesty, I learned more from the mistakes, and boy! Did I make mistakes! Some really big ones. I hope you find some of my experiences helpful as you think about boosting your team's performance through standards and expectations:

1. **Set** *a minimal level of performance and refuse to accept anything below it.*

2. **Spend** *the time training your team so they understand what needs to be done and what standards determine satisfactory performance.*

3. **Make** *sure that your team understands the consequences of performance that meets or exceeds your standards as well as performance that doesn't.*

4. **Recognize** *good performance as well as performance that does not meet the standards.*

5. **Reinforce** *the right actions on the part of your team. When they get that type of feedback, they will repeat their actions and encourage others to do the same.*

wannabes out there, remember that consistency builds trust, and trust is what leaders use with their followers.

Third, expect success from yourself and from others: Far too often, business leaders, including business owners, are way too tolerant of mediocre levels of performance. Some of you don't even set proper expectations for your team, and then you get angry when your team doesn't perform up to your nonstated standards. Get your head out of that dark spot! If you don't have standards, you have nothing to communicate and guess what? Your team has no guidance, and your business flounders. It's your fault!

Fourth, build a winning roster: Before you can set expectations for your team, you must have a team made up of the right people. Many bosses do not have a clear-cut description of whom they want to hire, the skills the prospects need to have, and how they should perform. I learned a long time ago that we tend to hire our own problems. Some of you even go into an interview without any idea of the questions you need to ask or how to evaluate the responses you get from the candidate. Yet, if they look good or have a neat resume, you hire them. Then—and here's the best part—ninety or so days after they join your team, they are not the same person you interviewed and they just don't seem to get it. Who hired them? You did, and you made a costly mistake. How costly? Well, if you make a mistake and hire the wrong person in a $50,000, mid-level, professional position, the cost to your company—after 90 to 120 days—would be approximately $20,000. Remember, to have an effective team, you need to have the right people with the right skills in the right roles at the right time. You have to set this standard and demand accountability to it. No exceptions.

Steinbrenner once said, "If you can't make tough decisions, then you can't be the boss." Leaders (bosses) know they have to make tough decisions. In most cases, they thrive on doing so. These decisions are often made quickly and based on less-than-perfect data. They know that hesitation can be deadly.

Fifth, Leaders Have a Vision or a Plan: They are able to communicate that plan to their team members and show them where each of them fits in. Leaders set the standard and hold the team accountable to meet those standards. Leaders never offer or accept excuses. They look for solutions and a way around problems. They do not shrink in the face of having to make a tough decision. When a leader does all of these things consistently and persistently, then and only then can he or she be called the Boss.

PLAY BIG: Being the Boss involves more than just having a big title. Make sure that your vision and goals are relevant and understood by all. To be the Boss you have to act like a great leader who sets great expectations for the entire team. What expectations do you have for your team?

Can You Really Manage a Crisis? You Bet You Can!

Henry Kissinger once said, "Next week there cannot be a crisis. My schedule is already full."

Oh, if it were only this simple. Imagine if you could plan when to have a crisis. Reality, however, sometimes gets in the way of the best plans in the form of a crisis, which by the way, usually comes as a surprise.

As we all know, you usually don't get the chance to plan a crisis. What you do get to do is to react to it. But there are good ways to react to it as well as some bad ways. A good way is to have a plan in place to minimize the impact of the crisis on you and your business. The plan, while general in nature, should be targeted to quickly bringing order to the chaos, to starting the development of a solution, and to identifying the opportunities that show themselves during the chaos.

A crisis has a way of damaging productivity within your organization. The key is to deal with it as quickly as possible to minimize the damage and get back on track. The bad news is that there is never a "last" crisis. The good news is that each one presents you with a unique opportunity to learn from it. This learning, when applied properly, makes you better and more resilient to handle the next surprise.

The Coach's Emergency Checklist

So, what can you do to effectively manage a crisis? Here are some steps that I have learned from my experiences:

1. Stop the bleeding quickly and get to work to minimize the disruptive effect it is having on your operations and services.

2. Assess the damage and get the facts. Ask questions of the right people so you can separate the clutter and fiction from reality.

3. With a better grasp of the relevant facts, you are now in an excellent position to dispel rumors, which always surface during a crisis, and communicate the next steps.

4. There is no time for emotion, excuses, or blame. The initial goal is to understand the real cause.

5. Begin to set expectations and accountabilities within your team regarding initial tasks. The goal is to get the team focused on stabilizing the situation. Make sure to solicit input from your team to help you set realistic deadlines for the completion of these initial tasks.

6. Let's not forget Murphy's Law. You know, if anything can go wrong, it will. In a crisis, multiply the likelihood of Murphy showing his face by a factor of ten. To combat this, work hard to keep your plan clear and updated. Practice—no, demand—quality communications and quick action when new surprises appear, courtesy of Murph.

7. Be seen and be heard. It is important that your team members see you involved as their leader. You want to make certain that you get 100 percent understanding and buy-in from your team on the job to be done. Communicate with your team as often as needed until all has been resolved and a sense of normalcy has returned.

As normalcy returns, begin to identify those things you would have done differently that would have allowed you to either prevent the crisis or handle it more quickly or effectively. Incorporate those findings that make the most sense into systems and procedures within your business. Make certain that your entire team understands these changes and is trained in their proper execution. Acknowledge the hard work of your team members during the crisis. Do whatever you must do to demonstrate to them that you are genuinely appreciative of their effort. Help them to learn from the experience so that they will be better the next time. And, rest assured, there will be a next time.

PLAY BIG: The most important aspect of a crisis is not the crisis. It is how quickly you can bring back order and eliminate confusion. What is your process? Can you execute it flawlessly? Does your team know it? Or, will you try to wing it? Create your plan now. Solicit input from your team to make the plan relevant.

You Have to Get the Cows Out of the Creek First

There is only one way to solve a problem: the right way.
—CHRIS RUISI

"Get the cows out of the creek" is an expression I first learned when I read an article about Meg Whitman, former CEO of eBay and current CEO of HP. She used the expression to describe her approach to problem solving. She analyzed and solved problems using a three-step process that should begin once you learn that you have a problem to deal with, namely, the cows are stuck in the creek and cannot get out.

Step 1: Get the cows out of the creek.
Step 2: Determine how the cows got stuck in the creek in the first place.
Step 3: Fix it to make certain that the cows don't get stuck in the creek again.

Let's discuss each step and my take on their meaning and application:

Step 1: Get the cows out of the creek: The first step addresses what must be done to start to move back to some form of normalcy in your operations. Clearly, while the problem persists there will be a continued disruption of operations and services. The company's money is either being lost or wasted. Future revenues may be at risk. An initial plan must be developed and implemented to stop its effect and start moving toward a solution to the problem. Get your team involved. Get their input. They are on the front line and have an upfront perspective. Put an initial plan in place to start collecting the facts so that duties and accountabilities can be assigned with short deadlines. This is not the time to rush into implementing any solution. You want to get the right information so that your eventual and permanent solution is right on target.

Step 2: Determine how the cows got stuck in the creek in the first place: The first step in correctly solving a problem is to understand fully its root cause. If you've handled it correctly, Step 1 should have given you most of that needed information. During Step 2, you will know in detail what the cause or causes were. Was it a procedural or business systems issue? Was there no system in place, or was the one already in place inadequate? Or, was it an issue related to poor training? Did the employee really understand what was supposed to have been done? Did someone try to cover up the mistake to avoid blame? Maybe, it was a customer-related issue? Was the customer given the right information? Did the customer not follow our instructions? There are many other questions that can and should be asked during Step 2. Dig deep to uncover the what and how of the problem. The goal is to end up with a firm grasp and understanding of what caused the problem.

Step 3: Fix it to make certain that the cows don't get stuck in the creek again: With Steps 1 and 2 successfully behind you, it's now time to focus on moving to a permanent fix so that the problem will not be repeated. This fix may involve a new system or procedure, a change in operations or employee training, or a restructuring of duties within a department or between departments. It might involve hiring new team members with different skill sets from those that already exist among your team members. What you've learned as a result of the problem must also be reflected in your fix or solution. We learn from our mistakes so long as we make the deliberate effort to apply that new knowledge to our business world. This will make you, your team, and your overall company stronger and better able to respond to the many new problems you will face in the future.

A question I am often asked is, "What is the best way to learn from our experiences?" My immediate response is, "Watch the game films." As I said earlier, watching the game films is a simple but highly effective process. Professional sports teams use this process daily and so can you. After a problem or surprise event ask yourself the following, "Based upon what we now know, if we had the chance to go through this experience again, what would we start doing, stop doing, do more of, and do less of?" I guarantee that if done correctly, this process will help you collect the right information to develop your permanent fix. Once you develop the fix, make certain that you include in your implementation of it comprehensive communications to your staff and, if applicable, to your customers so everyone understands what's been done, why, and how it will benefit them.

Finally, before you close the book on this experience, be sure you give credit to your team members for all of the heavy lifting they did to help you solve the problem. This is a critical last step that will pay you many dividends well into the future when you need that extra effort from your team again.

PLAY BIG: Develop your own approach/process to solve a problem the right way without wasting time. Identify the steps you will take to be proactive and focused in any problem-solving activities.

Don't Punish Your Best Performers!

When I discuss this problem, I refer to it simply as performance punishment. It's a slow but deadly process that can be found at one time or another in every business big or small, private or public, where weak managers work. By weak, I mean those who either have no people management skills or have them but do not know how to properly apply them. The symptoms are always the same: They will accept less than satisfactory performance to avoid confronting a problem, or they want to be liked by their staff as opposed to being respected.

The illness can exist in two different settings. In the first setting, it involves a better-than-average employee who is recognized as such by his or her superiors and peers and who works for a not-so-effective manager. The manager of this individual continues to pile on additional work, knowing that the individual has superior skills as well as a superior work ethic that does not allow him or her to say no or give up and can handle it until a certain breaking point is reached.

Because this individual is so valuable to the manager, the manager rewards him or her by giving this valuable employee more work, which in essence precludes the employee from earning or seeking promotional opportunities. The manager claims that the individual has a bright future with the company but just needs to wait a bit longer for the recognition he or she has already earned (until that breaking point is reached). Eventually, the superior performer realizes that his or her manager is weak and the subordinate's only course of action is to seek employment elsewhere—Yup! This is the breaking point. When the subordinate does offer his or her resignation, the manager is shocked and says, "I had no idea you were this unhappy. Why didn't you say something?" The subordinate is now faced with a choice: strangle the manager, or remain silent and offer to help the replacement employee's transition and just dream about strangling the manager.

Performance punishment can also exist when the superior performer carries his or her own workload along with the workload of a weaker/poor-performing teammate. In the early stages, weak managers punish the better performers, who already have a full plate, with additional work that weaker employees either cannot or will not do.

This usually begins when the weaker manager approaches the better employee with requests that sound like, "I know you're busy, but can you take care of this? [The weaker employee] just doesn't know how to do it." Or, "Can you handle

> ## COACH SAYS ...
> *Punishing your best employees is an illness that exists in far too many (failing) companies.*

this? We are pressed for time, and I know I can depend on you to get this done." Left with no choice, the better employee accepts the work and gets it done, plus everything else he or she is working on. How? Maybe the worker skips lunch or a break, or maybe works late several nights to avoid a backlog, or maybe both. The manager convinces himself he is a good delegator and the weaker employee goes home, on time, to his family.

The punishment escalates when the manager keeps coming back with additional work because he knows he can count on his better performer. Hence the vicious cycle of performance punishment is in place and destined to repeat itself until the better performer breaks, stops giving his or her best effort, and quits. In the meantime, the weaker performer continues the I-can't-do-this rant and gets to go home on time.

If ignored, the disease spreads everywhere at a rapid pace. The better performers reach their limit and quit. The poor performers solidify their positions and—get this!—get a raise and even a promotion and hire more people like themselves.

When this happens, the increase in poor performance eventually makes the paying customers mad, and they leave. The business suffers, and the owner and its managers scratch their heads and wonder why.

The Coach's Cure for Performance Punishment

From my experience, there is only one way to effectively deal with performance punishment. It is a multistep process.

1. The first step involves prevention. When you need to hire or promote someone, have a clear sight profile of the ideal candidate. This profile should include not only skills and experience needed for the candidate to be successful but also a description of the type of person who will fit into the culture of your company. Some of these things might include the candidate's work habits, interpersonal skills, and an ability to contribute to a team's success. Before you conduct an interview, have ready the questions that you will ask and a way to evaluate the responses. Ask some of your better performers to help you in the interview/selection process.

2. Once the candidate is hired, make sure you spend enough time to train him or her and put in place a process to measure when he or she becomes proficient. Many treat this type of training as a burden rather than one of the most important tasks a leader can do for not only the new employee but also his or her company. This initial training sets the foundation for performance expectations, or, in its absence, a future disaster.

3. Make sure that all of the members of your team know what they are supposed to do, how to do it (see #2 above), why they do it—namely how it fits into your company's purpose/operation—and how the performance of their duties impacts the jobs of their teammates and your customers—you know, the people who pay you.

4. Create a no-excuse culture within your company by setting expectations for your team members' job performance, and hold them accountable for meeting your expectations. Explain that mistakes are okay so long as they own up to them when they occur and learn from them.

5. Establish an employee-development meetings process (EDM) in your business and live by it. Meet periodically—maybe three to four times per year—with your team members and tell them how they are doing. If they are doing well, let them know. An EDM is also a good time to ask them for their input on business issues. Show them that you value their input. If they are not meeting your expectations, tell them that, as well as what they need to do to improve. The EDM

is in addition to your normal annual performance review program. In fact, when done properly, EDMs work to make the annual process more effective. Why? Because you are dealing with performance throughout the year. Even with the EDM process in place, you never wait to deal with significant performance issues when they occur.

6. Work with your managers to make sure that they are meeting your expectations and are implementing this multistep process within their own areas of responsibility. In order to get things done through their people, they and you need to pay attention to how they develop their teams.

7. Accept complete responsibility for the development of your managers. Help them to understand their role in making your vision a reality. Help them to see what they need to do to become leaders. Set the example for them.

If you follow this multistep process **consistently, persistently, and systematically**, you not only will increase productivity, but you also will make great strides to eliminate performance punishment from your company and create a healthy and productive no-excuse culture.

PLAY BIG:

As soon as you can, assess all of your best-performing employees based on their and your expectations. Are they being utilized to take full advantage of all their capabilities? Are they doing (carrying) work for others? If so, correct the imbalance. Take an equally hard look at those employees who are performing below your expectations. Determine why. Then, put in place a plan to help them improve their performance and level of productivity.

TO STEP UP AND PLAY BIG, YOU MUST STAY FOCUSED TO MAKE THE RIGHT DECISIONS

DON'T STOP LEARNING

This book is keyed to Leadership and other courses found online at Chris Ruisi's Play Big university at www.**StepUpandPlayBig**.com

The successful warrior is the average man, with laser-like focus.

—BRUCE LEE

Put Yourself in Time-Out

"That's it! You need a time-out!" This is a common expression that parents use when their child has either done something bad or is on the verge of doing something bad. I know. I have heard my son and daughter-in-law use it with our four-year-old grandson. I read the following on a parent help site: "Time-out is a very effective discipline technique." The key word here is discipline or, as you will read later on, self-discipline.

Time-out is also an action or tool that sports teams use to either take a breather to discuss where they are at a particular moment in a game, to discuss a possible change in strategy and/or tactics, or to slow down the surge or momentum of their opponents.

> ## COACH SAYS ...
>
> *Depending upon the sport, each team has a set number of time-outs they can use during the course of a game. Great coaches (leaders) know the best time to use them. When time-outs are used correctly and at the right time, it is not unusual to see a shift in the momentum of the game in favor of the team that called the time-out. The same holds true with four-year-olds.*

So, how does all of this matter to an executive or business owner? It's simple, really. A day doesn't go by that a business leader doesn't find himself or herself in a crunch, a crisis, off track, or overwhelmed. It comes with the territory and some believe like me that these types of situations test the depth of leadership and problem-solving skills. Some respond by plodding along at the same thing. Some even plod along at the same thing but at a faster pace. Others just get stalled, or distracted, and create another crisis somewhere else. Eventually, they all learn that their decision on how to handle the issue did not work, and they still have the problem. Usually it has gotten worse or out of control.

What would have been a better choice? Call a time-out. Take the time to evaluate the issue. See if you are still on track or need to make an adjustment to your game plan. Take ten minutes of uninterrupted time. This is really important, so that you can stay 100 percent focused on the issue. Plan out your next step in a logical way based upon the facts at hand. This is what winning teams do. The good news is that you have no limit on the number of times you can call a time-out. However, to call and use a time-out in an effective way, you must enhance your self-discipline skills.

STEP UP: If you find yourself constantly calling time-outs, you have a bigger and more serious challenge. You are probably lacking a vision, goals, any form of meaningful time management (you management) and planning skills. If that's the case, be honest with yourself and address it as soon as possible. Your business and your health hang in the balance. If you put it off, it will prove fatal.

What should you do now?

To get started, try this: During the course of the day, call a time-out every two hours and take an uninterrupted ten minutes to:

- **assess** what you are doing;
- **confirm** you are doing the right things; and
- **adjust** what you are doing so that it will get you closer to achieving your goals.

Make your last time-out of each day the time to assess how you did and to plan for the next day. If you can **build this habit over the next thirty days**, on a **consistent, persistent and systematic** basis, you will eventually no longer need to schedule your time-outs, although it's probably a good thing to keep on doing so but maybe not as frequently as every two hours. You will know when to call them going forward because you will have learned the skill and how to properly execute it.

If you follow the process I have outlined, you will find that the investment you make in time-out will be more than offset by increases in your own personal productivity and improvements in the way you lead your business. Think about it. You have nothing to lose. You probably waste ten minutes every two hours anyway. Why not recapture that time and turn it into an opportunity? It works in sports and can work for you.

Feel silly trying this? What's silly about doing things that will lead to more success?

PLAY BIG: Accept the fact that you cannot create more time. What you can do is determine the best way to use the time that you do have. Starting right now, schedule at least one, one-hour appointment with yourself each week. Go right to your calendar, pick a day and time that works best for you, make the appointment, and set it up as a recurring event. Determine in advance what you will work on during your appointment with yourself. Make sure it is something that allows you to work on your business.

Got Goals? Well, You better Have!

Brian Tracey, author of *Eat That Frog*, wrote: "Success equals goals; all else is commentary."

Every successful person I know or have read about has one important common characteristic. He or she has goals and uses those goals to achieve desired results. In fact, your life will take on real meaning once you begin to adopt a goals mentality and orientation. As I have said on many occasions, without goals, you are like a ship

Bench injuries

If having goals is so important, then why doesn't everyone have them? I can think of several answers.

- They just don't understand how important having goals is to their success. They think that they can go through life just winging it. Well, winging it gets you only so far. It's like being invited to watch a great party but not being allowed to go in.

- They don't know how to set real, meaningful goals, so they don't do it. By meaningful I mean specific, measureable, achievable, and realistic goals with a deadline.

- They fear failure. Failures hurts, but it can provide a valuable learning experience. Tennis champion John McEnroe captured it best when he said, "The important thing is to learn a lesson every time you lose." The other downside of being afraid to fail is that they get comfortable playing it too safe. When that happens, they hold themselves to lower expectations. The result is a quiet but deadly form of self-sabotage.

- They have convinced themselves that they just don't have the time to sit down and think about what their goals should be. Imagine someone who doesn't have the time to think about their future. They are destined to relive the mistakes of the past many times over into their future.

without a rudder, constantly at the mercy of the winds, waves, and currents.

STEP UP: The first thing you must decide is what is it that you want to achieve. Follow these steps to get started:

1. Set a specific goal that is important to you. Remember what I said before, it must be specific, measurable, achievable, realistic, and have a deadline.

2. Next, identify the resources you will need to achieve the goal. In most cases, this means time and money. It could also involve soliciting help from others. Asking for help from others is okay. There is no rule that says you need to do all of this alone.

3. Visualize what you want to achieve and think about how it will feel once you achieve it. Close your eyes and literally "see" yourself achieving the desired goal. The clearer this mental image is, the more likely it is you will achieve your goal.

4. Identify what, if any, obstacles you might encounter that could prevent you from achieving your goal. Think about how you will handle these obstacles.

5. From all that you have done so far, identify one to three possible ways that you could achieve your goal, taking into account the resources needed and the possible obstacles you may encounter. Then pick the best way to move forward.

6. Now identify all of the daily tasks you will need to undertake to achieve the goal. Organize them based on your timeline. Keep in mind that a number of little things done correctly and consistently result in big successes.

7. Finally, implement the plan and track your progress daily or as often as needed, adjusting your methods as you go. Remember, there is no backing down, but you can change course when necessary. Achieving the goal is paramount.

Winners spend a great deal of time thinking about what they want and what they have to do to achieve it. Wannabes are people who are envious of what others have accomplished, spend most of their time thinking and talking about what they are going to do, and then conclude that someone or something is standing in their way. You know, they do nothing and then they make excuses.

Those who take action on their goals are always learning and moving closer to achieving them. The wannabes live in the world of could have, would have, or should have. It's a horrible existence. As Napoleon Hill stated, "The primary reason for failure is that people do not develop new plans to replace those plans that didn't work."

So, with all of this as background, you should be asking, "Okay then, how do you go about identifying and setting goals?"

> ## COACH SAYS ...
>
> *One of the most basic components of success is that it doesn't matter where you are coming from. All that is important is where you want to get to. And, where you want to get to is reflected in your goals.*

PLAY BIG: The to-do here is really simple. Start setting goals and then work in a deliberate way to achieve them. Make sure each goal is specific, measurable, and realistic, and has a date certain to achieve it. To get started, identify a goal that meets the above criteria. Now, follow the seven-step process outlined here so that you will—not might—achieve it within ninety days.

Burn the Boats: Get Comfortable with Feeling Uncomfortable

There is a fable about a captain coming ashore to conquer a new land and finding his forces outnumbered ten to one. Seeing this, one of his officers asked what they should do, to which the captain replied, "Burn the boats."

Of course, this is a reference to the explorer Hernando Cortez. In the early 1500s he set sail from Cuba for Mexico with an army of six hundred men. To keep the men from retreating, he gave the order to burn the boats. The idea was that without any means to retreat, give up, or quit, they had no choice other than to be successful, or they would have no way to get back to their homeland.

> **COACH SAYS ...**
>
> *If you are going to achieve what you have a passion for, you just may have to burn the boats.*

Burning the boats assumes you have a vision and a focus that you are ready, willing, and able to unlearn old habits and replace them with those new habits needed for your success. This type of commitment will make most feel very uncomfortable. But, isn't that the real essence of change? To embrace change and leverage the full benefits it can bring, you will have to get comfortable with feeling uncomfortable.

Many people can talk a good game about the importance of change, but when they need to actually change, they head back to the "boats" as fast as their feet will carry them. Like Cortez, we need to burn our boats to eliminate any chance of retreat and any circumstances standing in the way of achieving our goals. Burning the boats highlights how strong your commitment is toward achieving your goals.

People without a vision, goals, passion, and commitment often complain that at the end of the day—as a result of undisciplined activity—they are burned out. I seriously doubt if they were ever on fire to begin with.

Get uncomfortable! Burn the boats!

PLAY BIG: Accomplishing big results requires big actions, which usually include some risk-taking. Also needed to achieve big goals is an unwavering belief in your abilities to succeed. Examine the last time you had to retreat to your comfort zone. What boat could (should) you have burned to allow you to not only stand your ground but to move forward?

Hey! Keep Your Eye on the Ball!

How many times have you heard that expression? Was it as kid at bat for the first time? It could have been any sport, really, in which one needs to focus on the ball. Or, maybe you've shouted it out to your child during a Little League baseball or softball game. Regardless of whether you heard it or said it, it is probably the universal call to pay attention, focus, and avoid distractions.

Clearly the phrase is applicable to a baseball or softball batter or fielder. How about in basketball at the moment when one player passes the ball across the court to a teammate only to see it slip through his hands and sail off into the seats? If you look at the replay, you can see the receiving player, for less than a split second, look elsewhere. Or, how about in football, usually in a long pass play when the receiver appears to be wide open as the ball leaves the quarterback's hand and sails to him? He's thinking that this will be one great catch and will be the replay of the week. Yup! You guessed! He took his eye off the ball for a second and it bounced off his chest or fingertips and rolled out of bounds. Another lost opportunity.

So, what does all of this have to do with you and your business or career? Heck, nobody is perfect 100 percent of the time. That's right, but I want to talk about those times when you wasted an opportunity

Bench injuries

In my experience, people take their eye off of the ball for several reasons:

- They either did not have a plan, or the one they did have was poorly constructed, lacking clarity about what was supposed to get done, by when, and by whom, and where it fitted in to the big picture.

- They did not have a comprehensive vision of what they were trying to create, with measurable benchmarks achieved over some specific timeframe. And, if they had no vision to begin with, they clearly had no plan. Do you see the relationship between a vision and planning?

- They thought that they could wing it. You know—make it up as they go. Winging it works only when it is really easy and there is no competition. In real life, there is no such thing as easy, and there is competition that would like nothing better than to eat your market-share lunch. So, the answer is to practice your craft until you can execute it flawlessly on a consistent basis under all types of conditions. Dick Buttons, the legendary men's figure-skating champion, once said, "If you practice the craft, the art will come." This is as true in business and leadership as it is in any type of sport.

- Finally, a lack of self-discipline is probably the single greatest reason for not keeping an eye on the ball. The leader who lacks self-discipline simply has not formed a strong enough habit to do the things he needs to do consistently, persistently, and systematically.

that should have been yours because you took your eye off the ball, namely, you allowed yourself to be distracted and lose your focus.

Keeping your eye on the ball, while fighting off all of the distractions in your way, is critical to your success. You can dramatically increase your chances of keeping your eye on the ball by having a clear and comprehensive vision of where you want to go, achieving that vision through accurate plans that are executed with discipline on a consistent, persistent, and systematic basis.

PLAY BIG: To keep your eye on the ball requires your full focus. What allows you to focus properly is the clarity of your vision and the goals contained within it. Once each quarter, re-evaluate your vision and goals for the coming ninety days. This exercise, if done consistently, will strengthen your ability to focus and hit the ball.

Is Hiring New Managers an Opportunity or a Future Problem?

When the economic recovery finally begins to gain traction, employers both big and small will be on the hunt for new talent at all management levels, up to and including the executive suite. The question is, will you hire the best person or a future problem?

But what are the characteristics of the best people you need to hire in order to improve business results and profitability? Remember that in addition to filling an open position, you are, in essence, building your future leadership team. The importance of whom to hire is now on the radar screen of many companies' boards of directors. Recently, the board of Bank of America, as a result of that company's continued mistakes and missteps, instructed the CEO to "hire and install people with experience and good judgment" in key roles (*Wall Street Journal,* 4/16/11).

Wow! "Hire and install people with experience and good judgment." How novel is that? Who wouldn't hire people with "experience and good judgment"? It appears that many have not sought these skills when building their executive teams. Experience and good judgment are, of course, key skills a manager or business leader needs to have. However, they cover a broad area.

STEP UP: Here's a list of key skills and traits that I believe business leaders need to possess to boost team performance and guide their company, big or small, public or private, to success. How many of these skills do you consider when you have to evaluate a new hire or a candidate for promotion?

They need to know how to manage the chaos that results in their finding opportunities to increase revenues and, in turn, profitability. They possess excellent execution skills. They know that a great plan executed poorly is a disaster. They focus on the details to get things done.

They are committed to **getting results.**

They are well rounded and understand the important role people play in the success of a company.

They understand the importance of investing in their people to give them the skills they need to succeed, the opportunity to use those skills, and feedback on how well they are doing.

They welcome risk and know how to assess it.

They have the ability to make "right" decisions with either incomplete or imperfect data.

They have demonstrated that they know how to create growth, even in a down economy.

They know how to capitalize on a company's uniqueness and create growth from it.

They **lead by example** so as to gain the respect of their superiors, peers, and team.

As I said at the beginning, these are key skills business leaders need to possess in order to increase their company's profitability and to be successful. There are others. But now that you know these, what are you to do? It's simple, really. First, have a plan when you need to recruit and hire someone. The plan should include a complete description of the person you need to hire, a comprehensive description of the role he or she will fill, the skills needed to properly execute the duties, what criteria will be used to measure satisfactory performance, the questions that you will ask, and a way to evaluate the candidate's responses.

There is an old expression that sums this up well: "Hire slow and fire fast." Take your time when hiring someone. However, if you made a mistake, deal with that fast before the mistake (the wrong person hired) causes harm within your organization.

One business leader, Barbara Corcoran, the real estate mogul and business consultant, has a very simple rule that she uses after she hires a new agent. It's "shoot the dogs early." If new agents don't produce revenue in their first sixty days, they are usually asked to leave. It may seem harsh, but every new agent knows exactly where they stand from day one.

PLAY BIG: While promoting from within is always the desired course to follow, it is sometimes necessary to bring in new managerial talent. When interviewing outside candidates—and even internal promotion candidates—what is the criteria you will be using to make the final selection? Develop that list right now along with the questions you will ask to evaluate each candidate's suitability. Where applicable, use assessment tools to help you in the evaluation process.

The Will to Win, Especially in Tough Times

If you are a business owner, at some time you will run into a tough economy. How tough? Tough enough that it might cause you to start thinking about either hunkering down until the storm passes, or worse: quitting and giving up.

Arnold Palmer once said, "The most rewarding things in life [and in business] are often the ones that look like they cannot be done."

Here are the steps that you need to take, things that you can and should do, to minimize your risk during the worst-case scenario:

1. Evaluate your cash needs for the balance of the year. Update your budget/plan and stick with it. If you don't have a budget, you are living on the edge already. Enough said!

2. Where possible, clean up and reduce your debt. Clean up your accounts receivable. Stop accepting every excuse for people not paying you on a timely basis. Stop playing the bank for these deadbeats. Not only do they have your money,

but they also are costing you more money and grief. Get cash in the door—now!

3. Fine-tune your marketing message and what makes you different. Downturns can be an excellent opportunity to build market share as others either hide or fail. But your message has to be clear and mean something to your buyers.

4. Re-evaluate your lead generation strategies to make sure you are spending your available time and money marketing in the right places—you know, those places where your ideal customer may show up. Stop! Did you hear me? Stop right now going to those useless networking events. I call them lonely-hearts clubs. Everyone has a story as to why things just are not that good. But no one has the courage to do something about it except you if you follow my advice. Right?

5. Get closer to your existing customers, the better ones. They will be your key to your continued viability during any prolonged downturn. Look to their buying patterns and be there to suggest reorders, purchases of other complimentary products you offer—you know, cross-selling and up-selling— and to solicit referrals. On the subject of referrals, you are not getting enough good ones. Why? You are probably not asking the right way. You have to do something about referrals right now! I use a proven process with all of my coaching clients.

6. Train your employees to understand your brand, what you do, and how it benefits your customers. Here's where you now think, "Come on, Chris, they know what we do." Yeah?

You think so? Set expectations on how they should perform internally and with your customers. Train them, I mean really train them. I have a very simple but effective approach that I use with my clients that outlines the right way to train your team. Your employees can destroy your customer base just by accident. Are you willing to take that risk and the consequences if you are wrong?

7. Set up a system that allows you to get the best ideas and feedback from your employees on improving the way you do business. Create a culture in your business that encourages your employees to solve problems and identify solutions.

8. Make sure that all of your programs, systems and procedures, where applicable, are responsive to your customers' needs. You want to make certain that your business consistently offers your customers a friendly, hassle-free experience.

9. Your job as the leader is to focus on only those priorities that will make a difference. Get it?

10. Read the first nine steps again. Make a copy and hang it in your office. Make another copy and keep it on your desk. Make a third copy and begin to discuss it with your team, soliciting their suggestions.

STEP UP: There is never a good time to give up, slow down, or hide until an economic

storm passes. As a business leader or owner, you have already successfully faced adversity in the past. We Americans, by our very nature, do not give up. We have learned to face adversity head-on and find ways to successfully push through it. It is our will to win that drives us. So, you have what it takes. Take your will to win out for a drive. Push the pedal to the metal and drive right toward your goals. You will need every bit of your perseverance and self-disciple to maintain control and focus on your journey. Success can be yours, if you want it and do the right things to achieve it.

The rule here is you never get ahead by following. Take the lead in every situation, including those that you may have brought on yourself, such as hiring the wrong person for a job.

PLAY BIG: There will always be tough times, but not everyone is ready to tough

them out. You will be, though, if you have in place a strategy before the tough times actually arrive. It will be too late to try to develop the plan after the serious challenges have begun. Use the guide described here to develop your plan now. Review it annually or as often as needed. Share it with your accountant and other advisors to solicit their input.

Five Great Ways to Run Yourself and Maybe Your Business into the Ground

Here are the top five ways business owners and even business leaders and executives can run themselves and their businesses into the ground. And, if they do all five, more than likely they will be unable to retain any good employees, an accelerant for burning the business to the ground.

As you read this list, be honest with yourself. If you are guilty of having any of these five traits, get rid of them as soon as you can. Here we go:

1. **Don't plan each day:** This is the number-one cause of wasted time, money, and energy. Now, why should you plan each day? It's more fun to live on the edge and operate in a defensive and reactive mode. You know who you are. You've convinced yourself that you can handle any crisis that comes your way. Let me let you in on a little secret: your lack of planning makes you the likely cause of the crisis. *Want to know what you should do?* Watch my rant titled "Show Me a Man or a Woman Who Excels at Putting Out Fires …" I'm talking about you in this rant. Having a daily plan, or even one for the week, gives you an edge. It gives you more control of your destiny. And, if a distraction pops up, your plan gives you the new starting point after you have eliminated the distraction.

2. **Don't train anyone else to do the tasks that you should *not* be performing:** Here's what you're thinking: "Come on, Chris, get real! I am great at announcing it will be easier if I do it myself." Well, that may be the only thing you are good

at. You're not good at planning, delegation, or developing your employees. *Want to know what you should do?* For starters, let me suggest that every time you feel the need to do something yourself, ask yourself if that would be the best use of your time. Ask also what would be a better use of this time. (Hint: grow your business. Look for new customers, etc.) If you have the time, I would urge you to read *The One Minute Manager Meets the Monkey* by Ken Blanchard. There is a very important message in this book for you. Stop doing other people's work for them, especially if you are also paying them.

3. **Don't have any clue as to the description of your ideal client:** Admit it. You really enjoy working with those customers who suck every bit of life and energy out of you. Plus, they probably want a discount on every sale and—here's the best—they pay you very, very slowly. At night you pray that the earth would open up and swallow them.

STEP UP:
If you don't have a description of your ideal client, how will you know where to look for him or her? If you don't know where to find him or her, you are probably wasting valuable marketing dollars and time.

Want to know what you should do? Ideal clients will inspire you, make you feel confident, pay you what you're worth, praise you, and refer other clients to you without being asked. One way of defining your ideal client is to look at past and present clients. Which of these clients did you enjoy working with the most? Pull those client files and list their common characteristics. Stop being a client victim!

4. **Don't deal with your poor performing employees:** It's easier to ignore them and ask your better employees to pick up the slack. Forget about the feelings of the better employees who are carrying their own weight plus the weight of the deadbeat. Some of you, to avoid dealing with them, will give them a lousy raise so they will quit—I never understood why you would give them a raise at all. But, they don't quit, do they? Why should they? They are doing the least amount of work and still getting paid! *Want to know what you should do?* Start learning the meaning of:

- performance appraisal
- setting performance expectations
- holding people accountable to meet your expectations
- following through with your team on the consequences of good performance as well less-than-acceptable performance

5. **Don't tackle the tasks you must do on a timely basis:** Be bold. Let the work pile up. It's more of a challenge to be a superprocrastinator and let the work pile up. Why? So you can complain about all the things you need to do. This approach is especially damaging when you put off working big projects that require several steps to complete. Your response: "Hi, honey, have dinner with the kids and kiss them goodnight for me. Don't wait up for me. Have to burn the midnight oil tonight to get some big project done that is due tomorrow.

Boy, I just don't know where the time goes. I'll probably have a burger at my desk and wash it down with some Red Bull." *Want to know what you should do?* Learn to break these big projects into smaller pieces. Tackle each smaller piece one at a time. *Eat That Frog* by Brian Tracy is an excellent source on how to stop procrastinating. Go buy it—now. You will be happy that you did. Next, develop and strengthen your self-discipline skills. The best definition of self-discipline that I have seen goes as follows: "Do what you are supposed to do, when you are supposed to do it, even though you don't feel like doing it.

All of these examples, if you do nothing about them, will run you and your business into the ground. You can always fix a business or start a new one. There is only one of you. *Want to know what you should do?* Stop the madness! You can if you want to.

PLAY BIG: Take each of the five examples given and identify—that means write them down—one specific action you will take over the next six months to elevate your performance and put an end to the madness.

CHAPTER 8

CREATING YOUR OWN STEP UP AND PLAY BIG DEVELOPMENT GROWTH PLAN—PUTTING YOUR STRATEGY INTO ACTION

DON'T STOP LEARNING

This book is keyed to Leadership and other courses found online at Chris Ruisi's Play Big university at www.**StepUpandPlayBig**.com

The big challenge is to become all that you have the possibility of becoming. You cannot believe what it does to the human spirit to maximize your human potential and stretch yourself to the limit"

—JIM ROHN, BUSINESS EXPERT

Making an ongoing investment in yourself to improve your skills is a requirement for anyone who wishes to step up and play big. To make certain that you get the return on investment in yourself mandates that you have a detailed plan to follow so that you can properly address and achieve your goals. The questions listed below represent an excellent starting point for your plan. As you begin to answer the questions, others may surface. Answer them. After all, we are talking about you, your future, and your success.

Your name: _____

Start Date: _____   Achievement Date: _____

1. What do you want to improve? What are your goal(s)?

2. Why? What are the consequences of doing nothing?

3. What new results do you want to achieve
   as a result of reaching this goal?

4. How will this change your performance, your career, or your business?

5. Explain why the achievement date is reasonable.

6. How will you go about doing it?

7. What are the steps you will follow and what order will you follow
   them in? (Attach another sheet if necessary. It's your plan.)

8. What resources will you need to be successful?

9. Who will help you, and what do you need to
   know in order to achieve this goal?

10. What obstacles and barriers will you face
    and how will you deal with them?

Here's What You Do Next:

Take your final goal, what you want to achieve, and

- establish goals for the first month following the start date you selected;
- from these monthly goals, establish specific tasks that you would plan to complete during each week of that month. Remember to set the right priorities;
- from the weekly goals, establish your plan for each day and select the number-one task for each day. Remember that you plan each day as your last task on the day before.

POST-GAME ANALYSIS
SOME FINAL COMMENTS

The last few years have constituted one of the most revolutionary business climates in history. I know that they rank right up there among the toughest and most challenging I have ever seen. Equally important is that these chaotic times of crisis have created what many have referred to as the new-and-still-evolving normal. During this new normal there will continue to be challenges and problems to be solved. However, what will make it even more interesting is that these challenges will have steeper peaks and deeper and more prolonged valleys.

As a business leader you will face challenges such as:

- periods of flat or, even worse, declining revenues
- adapting your marketing strategies during changing conditions without completely blowing your marketing budget
- keeping up with evolving technologies and their costs, which is needed for you to remain competitive
- finding and retaining the best employees while trying to avoid staff reductions
- building loyalty with demanding customers and clients who want more and more for less and less, and then some even take a long time to pay you
- many more challenges than can be listed here

This new normal climate will test every aspect of your leadership and business management skills. The burden will be on you to continue to learn new skills and enhance the ones you have if you want to succeed. All of these challenges carry with them make-or-break—business or personal failure—consequences.

> **COACH SAYS ...**
>
> *It's been said that knowledge is power. How you use that knowledge is more powerful.*

After you finish the book, or at any time during your reading, if you feel the need to do something about what you read, take that important first step toward becoming a master of your circumstances and stop being a victim. It's your time to **step up and play big.** Go for it. You have nothing to lose.

Make something happen today, and tomorrow, and the day after that, and so on, and so on.
—Chris "the Coach" Ruisi

CHRIS RUISI:
Inspirational and Motivational Business Speaker of Choice

Most speakers talk about how the world *should* work. Chris Ruisi talks about how it *really* works in a hands-on business, motivational and humorous style that delivers the solutions you need. His extensive knowledge and experience coupled with his quick humor help to keep an audience engaged and learning.

From his experiences in the corner office he has learned how to take the cards he was dealt and use them to his advantage. He has seen first-hand that if you don't adapt or stretch, you perish. Chris deals only with real-world perspectives to provide practical, real-time solutions.

He speaks the only way he knows, directly and truthfully, on how organizations work, how power works, and how decision-making works. It is this unique approach that makes Chris Ruisi one of the top business speakers in the market today. Chris addresses relevant issues that include:

- Showing your audiences how to take the right action
- Learning how to change the rules with honesty and integrity when confronted with a challenge or crisis
- Learning powerful personal strategies to discover your full capabilities and to shape your future

Here is what event planners and meeting organizers who have booked Chris as the keynote speaker at their event have said:

- *"All of our attendees left feeling energized and excited about the possibilities."*
- *"He provides a wealth of valuable information."*
- *"His genuine approach and personal interaction are things we could all emulate. Chris is sharp, funny, and well adjusted to communicate with any audience."*
- *"He has a way to drive home a message in an enjoyable fashion."*

The best motivational business speaker isn't necessarily someone who motivates or uplifts you. Many will have an impact that will only last for a few minutes. The best motivational business speaker will transport you into another time and place and can change your life with just a few, powerful, life-altering words. And that change is one that actually evolves and lasts.

Chris Ruisi is just this kind of motivational business speaker. Whether he is working an entire room of CEOs and business leaders, doing one-on-one business coaching, or sharing his experiences through his blog posts or videos, Chris leaves a lasting impact.

The real test of a great business motivational speaker is whether the audience leaves with more than they came in with. Take a look at what people have said after attending one of Chris's programs:

- *"The best speaker we have ever had."*

- *"He has the unique ability to make complex subjects simple to understand."*

- *"His real-life stories are what help to get his points across."*

- *"Chris put together one of the best programs I have attended in thirty years. I walked away with motivation and renewed energy."*

- *"Chris's seminar was a great learning experience. I arrived tired from a long day at work and left feeling energized and excited about the possibilities."*

Whether it's a presentation about embracing change, managing through chaos, leadership strategies, or the habits of a successful CEO, as a professional business speaker, Chris brings his practical and inspirational message to every audience that he has the opportunity to serve.

To book Chris to speak at your next event, call him at 732–275–9222. You can also learn more about him by visiting either www.**chrisruisi**.com or www.**thecoacheszone**.com.

To receive value and practical business advice from Chris, sign up at www.**tipsfromthetrenchesblog**.com.

Finally, you can connect with Chris in the following ways:
Linkedin.com/in/chrisruisi
Facebook.com/coachchrisruisi
Youtube.com/thecoachszone
Twitter.com/thecoachszone

ABOUT THE AUTHOR

CHRIS "THE COACH" RUISI

Chris began his twenty-five-plus years in the life insurance industry when he joined USLIFE Corporation in June 1974 as director of personnel. During his career at USLIFE, he held a number of executive positions as he progressed from vice president, human resources, to president and COO/CEO and member of the office of the chairman and board of directors.

Following the acquisition of USLIFE by American General Corporation (AGC), a $3 billion project he quarterbacked, he remained with AGC as president and CEO and member of the board of directors of two of its operating subsidiaries until May 1998.

As the founder and CEO of The Coach's Zone, Chris is an experienced business professional with an exceptional record of leadership. He mentors and guides executives and business leaders to find their "stretch" point to learn the full measure of their capabilities in chaotic times. He helps them to "master being comfortable feeling uncomfortable." He is also an accomplished and sought-after leadership/business motivational speaker, providing his audiences with direction and motivation on what is needed to accomplish whatever listeners set their sights on. He has extensive experience in getting the job done in areas impacting a company's success. His passion and desire to make a difference in the businesses and lives of the clients he coaches as well as the audiences who attend his engaging, educational, and inspirational presentations makes him "the Coach."

Chris is recognized as an experienced, results-driven executive with an exceptional record of achievement in teaching leadership, team development and mentoring, and creating and directing growth.

Chris Ruisi is

- **convinced**, from his own experiences, that it doesn't take as much effort as you might think to rise above the crowd and achieve success;

- **skilled** in helping others find their "stretch" point to learn the full measure of their true capabilities; he encourages those who want to perform at their maximum capabilities to master being comfortable feeling uncomfortable;

- **living proof** that failing and making mistakes provides the best platform for learning and self-development because you get the chance to assess what took place, and by using his unique watching-the-games-film approach, you recover and come back even stronger;

- **a seasoned competitor** who knows that the deadliest four-letter word in the English language is *can't* as it relates to the self-imposed limits we place on ourselves when we think we can't do or achieve something.

Chris understands how leadership works, how organizations work, how power works, and how decision-making works. Known as a popular blogger and sought-after speaker, he has also created an extensive video library on YouTube and a growing online "university" offering guidance, support, and instruction for those who want to learn the secrets of effective leadership and success. Through this work, he has created a community of entrepreneurs, executives and business leaders who understand the importance of stepping up and playing big.

One of his readers offered this quintessential description of Chris Ruisi: "Here's a guy who has made good decisions and bad ones and knows the difference. He consistently offers common sense wisdom and gives great advice, especially for those in a marketplace embroiled in chaos."

He is active in many community organizations. Recently, a video he funded and helped to create and produce, *Faces, Colors and Stories of Cancer*, received an award from the Jersey Shore Public Relations and Advertising Association.

Chris lives in Holmdel, NJ, with his lovely wife, Paula. They have been married for forty years and have had a fair number of fights. They have three sons, Christopher, Stephen, and Andrew, and are perfecting the process of spoiling their three grandchildren, Jonah and the twins, Olivia and Bennett, much to the dismay of their parents, Stephen and Mary. He and Paula enjoy deep-sea fishing in exotic places such as Costa Rica and Madeira. They have discovered that the secret to success in deep-sea fishing is to find a fish dumber and hungrier than they are. They are also the full-time caretakers—Yup! They clean up the poop—of their golden retriever, Riley Rose, a certified Canine Good Citizen and Therapy Dog, and Toby, their West Highland white terrier, recently relocated from Florida.

Printed in the USA
CPSIA information can be obtained
at www.ICGtesting.com
JSHW012035140824
68134JS00033B/3073